RAMBLING RETIREMENT REFLECTIONS

After Forty-five Years On the Faculty
of Christopher Dock Mennonite
High School

S. Duane Kauffman

Art, Thanks for the memories of those early days.

[signature]

A Christopher Dock Mennonite
High School Publication

CD
CHRISTOPHER
D•O•C•K

RAMBLING RETIREMENT REFLECTIONS
After Forty-five Years on the Faculty of
Christopher Dock Mennonite High School

International Standard Book Number: 0-9741020-2-4

Library of Congress Control Number: 2004108351

Design and publication services by PMT, Ltd.,
Harleysville, PA 19438

Printed in the United States of America.

TABLE OF CONTENTS

PREFACE

Just as the schoolmaster Christopher Dock would not have published his 1770 *Schul Ordnung* (School Management) without the insistence of the Philadelphia printer, Christopher Sauer, S. Duane Kauffman would not have published his 2004 memoirs without the insistence of his colleagues and family. Dock did not want to create a "monument" to himself, and Kauffman steadily resisted doing the same. However, in finally agreeing to write his teaching autobiography, Kauffman has modeled the three *habits of mind* that under gird the educational program of Christopher Dock Mennonite High School in the 21st century, the ability to *Reflect*, to *Articulate*, and to *Demonstrate*.

To reflect means to revisit and make sense of an experience. To articulate is to speak with clarity, and to demonstrate is to show. This tome revisits 45 years of teaching in the high school classroom and speaks with clarity, demonstrating how some of life's experiences make sense only through the lens of maturity, after one's hair has turned from chestnut brown, to silver, to almond tree-blossom white.

Many who read these reminiscences will discover what the author himself readily admits: "Apparently much of my external expression belied my real nature." I well recall the moment when I first realized in Duane what Shakespeare called "seeming versus being." It happened during my first time at the biennial Mennonite Secondary School Teachers' Conference at Laurelville in 1979, when several hundred educators filed into the dining room to find places to sit. While standing in line with Duane, I realized that this would be the first of several times over those three days that my former teacher and now colleague would rely on me to make him socially comfortable. Until that weekend it had not seemed possible that this master of his domain could be so shy and reserved outside of the classroom. That genuine shyness remains with him to this day.

Students who knew Duane in the early years of his long tenure will hear the voice of an insecure, crew cut rookie who would later wish that he could give tuition refunds to his first students. Those of us who sat under his tutelage in the early seventies will hear the booming voice of a seasoned, pedagogical revolutionary; and those who were his students and colleagues in the 80s and 90s will hear the voice of the elder statesman whose opinions and counsel were sought but rarely given without solicitation.

Though *Schul Ordnung* portrays and preserves the spirit of the man who wrote it, the value of that treatise, beyond the local community, lies in the articulated rules, beliefs, theories and practices that shaped Dock's unusual approach to curriculum and instruction. Duane Kauffman's reflections, while narrating the development of an extraordinary educator, also offer specific rules, beliefs, theories and practices that shaped his life both inside and outside of the community while living the life of a "24/7" educator. His former students and colleagues will enjoy analyzing the rationale behind his approach to running a classroom, and trying to identify some of the students he cites by first name only. Beginning and veteran educators will benefit by comparing and contrasting their own philosophies with that of the one who, according to a *Schul Andenken* photo caption: "Looks like Santa Claus. Sounds like God."

Regardless of the audience for this memoir, it is fitting that the school's half century review includes the insights of one who was there to witness almost all fifty years, recording them with the eye of Herodotus and heart of Christopher Dock, himself.

J. Eric Bishop, Class of 1974
and CD Faculty since 1978
Souderton, Pennsylvania
March 2004

INTRODUCTION

Father's Day 2003 was a very special occasion for me. At that time over a hundred members of the Christopher Dock High School family gathered to celebrate my forty-five years of service and to wish me well as I began my retirement journey. In her concluding remarks, Principal Elaine Moyer said, "One thing you could give back to the school would be to take some time in writing your memoirs. On behalf of the school and extended community, that would be a real gift to us all."

Though I did not dismiss the idea entirely, I did not give it serious consideration at the time. I wasn't sure I had anything worthwhile to say. Also, I have always been somewhat suspicious of autobiographies that seem to be either egocentric splurges or bouts of masochistic self-flagellation. After some further prodding and my wife's suggestion that doing it might help to bring closure to my Christopher Dock experience, I decided to take up the challenge. The decision was clinched when I considered the potential of providing an insider's view to supplement the written history being published to commemorate Christopher Dock High School's fiftieth anniversary.

Hopefully my work will be of general interest, but my primary focus was on providing something that would be helpful to my fellow teachers. In attempting to provide an honest portrayal of my CD experiences, I have decided to make myself vulnerable, and some disclosures may alter some established perceptions. Since I had no diaries to which I could turn, I had to depend almost exclusively on my memory. Passage of time has warped my sense of progression, so instead of a chronological narrative, I have chosen to tell my story with a series of topical vignettes.

I would like to acknowledge Principal Elaine Moyer for encouraging me to take on the project, Eric Bishop for his editorial assistance and willingness to write the preface, and my wife Naomi for her helpful suggestions and understanding during my preoccupation with the task. I would also like to thank Mark Tuttle for assuming responsibility for publication on very short notice. Most of all, I would like to thank all who have made my Christopher Dock experience so rich and rewarding.

Duane Kauffman
April 2004

R
R
R

I. CHOOSING A CAREER

"Some day I am going to be a preacher like that!" According to my mother that is what I proclaimed at age eight in the family car as we returned from church where an eloquent evangelist had held sway. She was convinced that this was the manifestation of an early divine call, but her motherly pride was gradually diminished when, unlike my father, grandfather, and great grandfather, it was not my lot to be ordained to the preaching ministry.

It is true, I have never been granted credentials for serving as a pastor of a congregation, preaching Sunday sermons, or giving the invitation at revival meetings. Yet, as a lad, little did I know that the time would come when as a classroom teacher my demeanor and message would at times be much like that of a pulpit-thumping preacher or even one of the prophets of old.

Though I harbored some secret thoughts of becoming an auctioneer, I do not recall ever saying, "I want to be this or that when I grow up." I certainly did not see teachers as fortunate persons with enviable positions to which I would aspire. If anything, I saw them as poor souls who had been cursed by their entrapment in some strange scheme of things. As a child, becoming a teacher was very far from my mind.

Like most of my classmates at Bratton Township consolidated Elementary School I assumed farming was my destiny. When I was eight, our family moved onto a farm that my parents had rented. As the oldest child a significant portion of the chores became my responsibility. Though Dad's demands at times seemed unreasonable, I took things in stride, neither relishing my role nor detesting it. Activities such as cranking the old Fordson, mucking out stables, feeding the threshing machine, washing Beauty's udder, pulling out reluctant calves, disinfecting chicken coops, and leading the bull to the creek to drink not only helped to build character, but also provided a plethora of illustrations for later classroom use.

After graduation from eighth grade I went across the river to Bratton, McVeytown, Oliver, Joint High School (later named Rothrock in honor of McVeytown's forest and conservation hero). There participation in the band and orchestra was so important that those who played musical instruments were given schedule privileges and considered to be the academic students. Since I did not receive instrument instruction I found myself with the ordinary non-academics who tended to merely put in time. In grade ten I enrolled in Belleville Mennonite School on the other side of Jack's Mountain. Though I received spiritual nourishing and developed invaluable friendships with caring teachers and students, the educational program was less than challenging and did little to foster a desire to continue academic pursuits.

By the time of my senior year, my parents had dropped frequent hints that they expected me to go on to college. When I questioned the financial feasibility of such a venture they assured me that my Aunt Bernice was willing to loan me the necessary funds. Even after I agreed to give college a try I had given little thought to my choice of a life vocation. That changed after my high school senior interview. In the course of the conversation, Principal Zook effectively affirmed my potential and urged me to consider the teaching profession. A short time later Bishop Glick impressed upon me the opportunities in teaching as a type of mission service. Admittedly the observation that my two uncles, who were doing better than my other relatives economically, were both teachers did not escape my attention.

In the fall of 1954 I enrolled in the Bachelor of Science in Secondary Education program at Eastern Mennonite College in

Harrisonburg, Virginia. There was never a doubt about the choice since my father and even my paternal grandmother had spent some time at Eastern Mennonite High School. Predictably, in my first experience away from home I found plenty to do that provided stiff competition for my academic priorities. Though I had managed good grades in high school with a minimum of effort, I found the college situation to be quite different. My parents were deeply troubled about the results sent home on my grade reports. Of even greater concern was the number of "quality points" deducted for skipping chapels and unexcused absences to class.

By my third year in college I had developed somewhat of a reputation. However, it was not for scholarship or student leadership. I had become a marginal student who identified with those whose names were found on the prayer lists of the faculty and concerned students. Our misbehavior consisted primarily of rebellion against some of the ultra-strict policies of the day such as the requirement to sign out every time we left campus and dealing with the challenges of the ten o'clock curfew. Our worst transgressions were attending community all-night southern Gospel quartet rallies and occasional treks to Elkton to the movies.

One thing that brought me positive recognition was my musical involvement, even though that "raised a few eyebrows" at times. My ability to reach low notes secured me a place in the college choirs, men's quartets, and for a while on a Mennonite Hour octet. These opportunities brought fulfillment and the various tours broadened my horizons considerably. At the same time however, I was involved in another genre of music.

On one occasion Brother Yoder said, "I have heard of such a thing as tomfoolery, but now I see there is also "duanefoolery." This was a response to hearing my roommate, coincidentally another Duane, in one of our entertaining performances. It had become a regular late-night event for our dorm room to burst at the seams from the audience listening to our repertoire of folk

songs along with some original compositions. Eventually we even
progressed to broadcasting over the radio with a borrowed crys-
tal set. With guitar and ukulele accompaniment, songs about
stubborn cats, wrecked trains, penitent prisoners, and dying
infants were interspersed with commercials plugging *Mother
Murphy's Medicated Meatballs*, *Never Lasting Tombstones*, and
Aunt Eliza's Spot Remover "that not only removed the spot, but
the thing that had caused the spot, and the place where the spot
had been." Our most enduring legacy, without a doubt, was our
version of Homer and Jethro's parody *Movin' On,* which we
transformed into the 30 stanzas of the *EMC Faculty Minstrel
Song.*

During my junior year I finally became more serious about
my academic program. I even shocked many people by making
the honor roll for the first time. It was amazing how that success
bred more success! Without a doubt, the major reason for my
transformation was my future wife Naomi Hoover with whom I
was going steady. I felt motivated to get my act together in order
to measure up to her expectations. She was so studious that many
of our weekend dates consisted of studying together in the college library. More important, having her as part of my life added
a dimension that gave me a brighter outlook on things.

As a senior I roomed with John, a BMS schoolmate. His
commitment to making it into medical school set a disciplined
tone in our room that was conducive to serious study. The two
of us also became part of a team that made a 25-mile trip on
Sundays to a small mountain mission in West Virginia. My role
as a Sunday school superintendent and teacher was invaluable in
terms of my spiritual growth and leadership training. Here I
experienced the satisfaction that came from planning and providing activities that provided young boys with opportunities to
learn by exploring and discovering.

During my last semester I actually discovered what it was like
to "burn the midnight oil." In addition to regular courses, I was
doing my student teaching, which involved a class in General

Biology and another in American History at Eastern Mennonite High School. At this point I paid the price for my earlier lax approach to the mastery of subject content. With the help of my supervising teachers and understanding students I met the requirements. However, down deep inside, I had misgivings about the prospects of being hired as a teacher and wondered what I would do if I were ever offered a job.

2 SERVING GOD AND COUNTRY

It was my expectation, as well as that of my many others, my mother most certainly included, that my teaching career would be launched at my alma mater Belleville Mennonite. But, by March of my graduating year the only possibility there was an anticipated opening in science. Though I would have been comfortable with General Science and Biology, the Physics and Chemistry made the package far less attractive. During the first week in March of 1958, I received my first letter of inquiry. It was from Pigeon, Michigan where a Mennonite elementary school had recently been started. The offer was for a position as an eighth grade teacher, but along with that was the frightening responsibility of also being the principal of the entire school.

Several weeks later, I received a letter from Richard C. Detweiler, principal of Christopher Dock Mennonite High School inviting me to consider the possibility of teaching there. My interest was sparked immediately because I had some previous knowledge about the school. It was the place where my BMS English teacher Edgar Clemens had gone when he answered the call to become part of their faculty in order to start a new Mennonite school in his home community. I also remembered being impressed when the campus with its stately white columned building was pointed out as I was on a tour with the Big Valley Men's Chorus. The position offered was a combination of General Science, Problems of Democracy, and Pennsylvania History and Civics.

This opportunity seemed almost too good to be true, and my choice was made easier by the discovery that the school was on a list of non-profit institutions approved by the Selective Service Act as acceptable options for alternative service for conscientious objectors. Though uncertain as to whether I would ever be drafted, this opportunity seemed too good to pass up. After indicating my interest in pursuing the offer, I was sent an application form, which in addition to questions about my educational and occupational background included a set of questions calling for a written expression of my Christian testimony and a response to issues such as evolution, "headship," and attire.

One night in early April I was surprised by being called to the telephone near the dorm lounge. The voice at the other end introduced himself as Elmer Kolb, a member of the Religious Welfare Committee at Christopher Dock High School. He went on to say that they were satisfied with the way I had responded to the questions on the application form, but that there was considerable concern about my appearance in the accompanying photo. They were hesitant in giving approval for my hiring because of my necktie and fashionable hairstyle commonly known as a crew cut. After considerable, but amiable, conversation, we reached an understanding that I would wear a required plain coat, and though they preferred a more traditional haircut, that matter would be left to me.

Later that month, before my official hiring, I found myself on the CD campus as a member of EMC's Alleluia Singers. After our performance I was surprised when several students who had somehow gotten the word, greeted me as one who would soon be a new teacher on the CD faculty.

After my graduation from Eastern Mennonite College in May of 1958, while their school was still in session, I made another visit to the Christopher Dock campus. As it turned out it was not a typical school day since many of the students had gone on an end-of-year outing. After a pleasant lunch at the home of Board President Paul Clemens, I had an interview with

Principal Detweiler. He not only confirmed my appointment, but also gave me the good news that they had replaced General Science with Physical Education on my teaching schedule.

My 1-W commitment called for 24 months of service and since school terms were only nine months long, Mennonite Central Committee had to work out a plan for the time when school would not be in session. I decided to begin my service assignment in June before the September opening of school. As a result I found myself serving as a counselor at Mennonite Youth Village near White Pigeon, Michigan. Though I would have benefited by using my summer in classroom preparation, my days at Mennonite Youth Village proved to be a good experience. I learned a lot about myself. I enjoyed the camaraderie and teamwork of the staff and found fulfillment in relating to the kids who delighted in their camp experiences as they enjoyed a respite from their urban environment. Three days after my summer voluntary service had ended I was sitting at a table on the second floor of the Christopher Dock Science Building for faculty in-service. The stage was set.

3. ROCKY THE ROOKIE

Though some confidently move into teaching, and seem to master the challenges well, such was not the case for me. I got off to a shaky start. My first involvement with the student body was the frightening experience of leading a song for our first chapel worship. Principal Detweiler knew I had sung in choirs and quartets and assumed I could lead singing. What he didn't know was that my vocal range made it difficult for me to sing the melody in the pitch in which the song was written. Out of a sense of duty, with quivering falsetto and shaking hymnal, I struggled through *O Master Let Me Walk With Thee* and He did not let me down. I survived the moment but in all my years at CD I never led the student body in another song.

My first class was senior POD (Problems of Democracy) on the second floor of the Administration Building (now known as Detweiler House). As I walked into the room "Terry the Terror", a mischievous lad who had been a "thorn in my flesh" during my days as a student teacher at Eastern Mennonite High School, and had now migrated to Montgomery County to haunt me, raucously greeted me. I proceeded to call the roll. When I called out "Donald", Ernest responded. For Robert, Donald responded and for David, John said, "present". Finally much too late, a ripple of classroom laughter made me aware that "I had been had." Needless to say, the wee bit of confidence that I had successfully mustered was greatly dissipated.

Today as I think back over my early teaching days I am
appalled by my approach and obvious shortcomings. As a naïve
and insecure rookie teacher I was convinced that the ultimate
goal was to be liked by the students. I was inclined to do things
their way and to avoid actions that might evoke negative
responses. I tended to see myself as one of them. This was not
difficult since I was unmarried, had the crew cut that was in
vogue, and was only four years older than some of them. And
being somewhat of a country bumpkin, I perceived some of
them to be more worldly-wise than I was. Students chose their
own seating arrangement and I refrained from dealing with tardiness and classroom disruptions. I went with the flow and as a
result there were some difficult rapids to negotiate. Fortunately a
strong core of conscientious and caring students prevented things
from ever reaching a state of chaos.

The classes of 1959 and 1960 both had a clique of male students whose attitudes and conduct presented demanding challenges for the teachers and administration. In the senior class there
were Ernie, Don, Bob, and Dave who was better known as "Curly."
The juniors also had their Ernie and Don, along with "Whitey"
and Henry. Though they were more mischievous than malicious,
their rowdiness at times was obnoxious and destructive. That
these rascals were all "general" and "commercial" students was no
coincidence. Compared to the "academics," they lacked status
and were denied privileges that most certainly bred feelings of
inferiority and bitterness. I happened to be one convenient outlet
for their frustrations. Though later, Dave would claim that I
owed them a debt of gratitude for their favor of breaking me in,
their real motivation was certainly less noble than that.

During the first day of school and the days to follow I
became aware of the fact that I was christened with a new name.
When I was at an appropriate distance they referred to me as
Rocco, which later became *Rocky* or just plain *Rock*. Eventually in
their boldness they even addressed me that way. I could never
figure out their strange choice. (This was long before Sylvester

Stallone, the motion picture hero, had arrived.) At my 2003 retirement reception Dave admitted he was not sure of the reason for the selection but went on to say that he thought it had something to do with my rocking gait or my low rocky voice.

Another interesting practice that became contagious was for students to play on the name Kauffman by engaging in a round of coughing when I was around. Along the way I sat on my share of well-placed thumbtacks, sought long and hard for vanished grade books, removed embedded chalk from my erasers, and answered 2:00 AM phone calls. Though years later I would have dealt with such disrespect with a firm hand, I saw such developments as innocuous and took them in stride. Maybe it even made me feel more like "one of the boys."

It seemed that most of the gang were mechanically inclined. My '49 Ford coupe bore the brunt of a number of their pranks. Some were simple such as letting the air out of the tires and hiding the valve stems, jacking up the back wheels and putting the axle on blocks, writing slogans on the windows with soap, or clogging the door locks with chewing gum. One of the more dramatic ventures was the installation of a "car bomb." This was an explosive device attached to a spark plug wire that gave the gathered audience great satisfaction when the driver was horrified by the deafening blast. On one occasion the rotor was removed from my distributor. After almost draining the battery with my futile efforts to start the car, Bob appeared feeling smug and superior since he was able to help me in my distress. What Bob never knew was that I ended up with a significant garage bill since the incident put the timing out of whack.

On one occasion I even received money to buy a new shirt. I was umpiring a softball game and Henry threw a firecracker designed to fall behind me and explode. Unfortunately, it landed on my back, staying there long enough to burn a hole in my shirt before it was harmlessly extinguished.

Perhaps my willingness to accept the harassment was due partly to the fact that my own high school record was quite similar to that of my tormenters. This background gave me the ability to understand their motives and modus operandi and gave me a greater capacity for tolerance. Then too, deep down inside I, no doubt, had a strong suspicion that God was following through with His principle of sowing and reaping.

My attendance at Belleville Mennonite High School was due partly to my parents' concern about some of the public school influences to which I had succumbed. At BMS I did not give my best effort efforts academically and engaged in more than my share of misbehavior. I had developed a knack of attaching "car bombs" that others had provided. I remember several foolish incidents of skipping class. In one case a number of us spent time in the broom closet when we were supposed to be in class. My closest call to suspension came from a time when Jesse and I decided to take the afternoon off and explore the Ore Bank instead of going to Bible class. What happened upon return has been forever etched in my memory. We were greeted by a teacher, who with red face and bulging veins, dramatically exclaimed, "There is one thing I know, and that is that both of you will spend some time in the penitentiary before you die!" (This same teacher was the first one hired when Christopher Dock High School was started and was therefore a colleague of mine on the faculty for a number of years.)

One of my most disconcerting first year memories at CD involved a problem of locker room larceny. On a number of occasions sums of money had been stolen from wallets of boys taking gym. A number of seniors who had been victimized took it upon themselves to track down the culprit and bring justice by marking some bills and setting them out as bait. Sure enough, the money disappeared. During the activities period later that day there was a knock on my classroom door and four or five senior boys took charge by announcing that the girls were to be dismissed and all the boys were going to be searched even if it meant stripping. Though they assured me they had received administrative approval for the procedure, I felt something was amiss. All I could do was to meekly stand by while they began to initiate their proceedings. As it turned out the complete search did not prove to be necessary because one of the freshman boys was observed placing something under the heating radiator and was subsequently revealed to be the person they sought.

Strange as it may seem, on several occasions I actually "buddied" around with several of the senior boys who caused me grief. (Though I was single, I was engaged at the time so I never dated any of my students or any other girls in the community.) I remember distinctly an occasion at the end of the school year when I went out with Don, Dave, Bob, and I think Orrie, though he was an "academic". After a round of miniature golf at Montgomeryville, Bob gave me the fright of my life when he put his Olds 88 up over 100, which was faster than I had ever gone in a car before or since. That was the last time for anything like that!

Though teaching colleague Edgar Clemens was the only person I knew when I moved to the Bucks-Mont area, my sense of loneliness was minimal. Spending the first week in the home of Principal Richard Detweiler helped to facilitate a smooth adjustment. I then had the good fortune of finding lodging in the home of Jacob and Ruth Rittenhouse near the Plains Mennonite Church. There I was treated like a son as Ruth, in particular, went out of her way to cater to my needs and wants. Jake, the preacher at the Lansdale Mennonite Church, had a reputation for his conservatism and strictness and I knew I would have to "walk the line" since he was one of the three members of the CD Religious Welfare Committee a body charged with being the school's spiritual watchdog. The religious tone in the home was very similar to that in my family home. One of the features was eating breakfast together and after the meal listening to the reading of a passage of Scripture followed by kneeling around the table while each person offered a prayer. Embedded in my mind is the memory of how Ruth would always end her prayer by saying, "And do not let us become weary in well-doing." By providing security and expectations, the two years in the Rittenhouse household were very important in my maturation and adjustment to life in the North Penn Valley and Christopher Dock High School.

My most positive memories of my first year grew out of my association with the Class of 1962 of which I was the advisor. Since we were all new to the school, we were in the same boat. We struggled together and had a mutual understanding that led to cooperation and support. As their advisor for their entire four years I developed friendships that are precious to this date.

Class of 1962 Fortieth Year Reunion
First Row, left to right: Judy Schmell Gerber, Lorraine Alderfer, Phil Moyer. *Second Row:* Sylvia Moyer Derstine, Mary Lou Weaver Houser, Lucy Clemmer Gahman, Gladys Derstine Stutzman, Miriam Bauman Allison. *Third Row:* Elaine Kulp Worthington, Esther Stoltzfus Rittenhouse, Nancy Mininger Landes, Emily Derstine Walson, Duane Kauffman, Rhoda Alderfer Kauffman, Sara Lapp Kolb, Ruth Ann Hackman Kulp, Pearl Schrack. *Fourth Row:* Janet Martin, Vic Myers, Lester Kolb, Herb Myers, Jim Halteman, Noah Kolb

4. GAINING COMPETENCE

A competent teacher must have respect and confidence. Respect is not granted automatically as an inherent element in the noble teaching profession. It is not even bestowed as an initial anointing that serves during a time of probation for as long as it is merited. No, it is something that is gradually earned by demonstrating qualifications that in the minds of colleagues and students pass the test. Before others grant respect it is imperative that the teacher has respect for himself. Only then can the teacher reach a point of confidence in his ability to perform. Respect and confidence are inseparable. Without confidence there can be no self-respect, and it is also true that respect for one's self is an absolute prerequisite for confidence.

One of the keys to developing competence is the ability and willingness to learn from experience. This means avoiding patterns that were detrimental and continuing those that have been positively productive. After reflecting on my first year's tribulations, I made a firm commitment to be more assertive in maintaining discipline. This included a firm hand in classroom management by using a pre-determined seating plan and being more aggressive in dealing with classroom disruptions.

Another important decision was to do away with the "buddy-buddy" stuff and maintain more distance between the students and myself. I was determined that there would be no more name-calling or auto tampering. As it happened I did not have to take any drastic steps. The four rowdy seniors were no longer around to torment me. And as a result of maturity and increased confidence, I did not seem as much a "Rocco" as I had before.

A major factor in the development of more self-respect was finding acceptance in the local community. Much of this came from my involvement in a local congregation. Since I had boarded with the Rittenhouses, it was natural for me to attend Lansdale Mennonite, a small congregation where Jacob was the pastor. I found fulfillment, as I got involved in teaching Sunday school and participating in Sunday evening sessions of Bible study.

After marriage and subsequent move to the Perkasie area, my wife and I became members at Perkasie Mennonite where Principal Richard Detweiler was pastor and several other CD teachers attended. There we became part of a church family to whom our commitment has remained to the present time.

During my second year several men from Lansdale Mennonite convinced me to join them and become part of the Penn Valley Male Chorus. Singing in this ensemble under the direction of J. Clyde Landes was a highlight during my first decade in the Bucks-Mont area. About the same time, I accepted an invitation to sing bass in a men's quartet created to be part of a new radio ministry known as the *Life With God* program. In addition to recording for the regular broadcasts, we accepted invitations to sing for other occasions in the community. I formed valuable friendships in the choir and quartet and received exposure in the broader community.

Certainly my marriage to Naomi Hoover in June 1960 after my second year at Christopher Dock contributed significantly to my teaching competency. Not only was Naomi a settling influence, but also as a public school teacher she provided inestimable understanding and support. This has continued to our retirement days despite some philosophical differences arising from her commitment to public education while I have been convinced of the case for Mennonite schools.

During my first several years I suffered the frustrations common to teachers who are called to teach something about which they know very little. I found myself doing research the night before to stay one jump ahead of students in the next day's class. In order to avoid embarrassment and disgrace, I followed lecture notes closely, deliberately discouraging class participation that would expose my ignorance. Students have an uncanny ability to detect shallowness and phoniness. That being the case, I soon learned not to try to bluff my way through when I came up short, but to admit my lack of knowledge with a promise to check it out or by asking a student to find the information. Though this was honorable and sound educationally, too many of these occasions tended to threatened credibility.

In the final analysis, my competence improved only after I obtained sufficient knowledge of my subject field. This came from the opportunity to teach the same material year after year, but mostly the progress was a result of additional course work. My shortcoming was due partly to my cavalier approach to academics during my early college days. It was also a result of my inability to narrow my college major to one particular choice. This resulted in certification in both biology and history but my mastery of the content in both was marginal at best.

After the conclusion of my first year, I took advantage of a scholarship and enrolled in a summer program at Eastern Baptist College. My 1-W commitment called for me to work forty-hour weeks in campus maintenance in order to meet summer service expectations. To meet this requirement I had to work in the evenings until dark as well as on Saturdays. Despite the full schedule, I found my first graduate school experience to be positive and I was motivated to enroll in a Master's program at Temple University in Philadelphia. By commuting down town and taking evening and summer classes I managed to get my Masters of Arts in History in June 1963. The routine was extremely grueling as I tackled three or four class preparations at CD in addition to graduate school classes. To gain acceptance into Temple's graduate program I was required to compensate for my academic shortfall by taking additional courses in geography, sociology, and political science. However the real pressure came from being accepted conditionally with the understanding that I would be allowed only two courses with a grade of C or less. Unfortunately I used up my quota after my first three classes, which created an intense awareness that if I received one more C it was all over.

After completing my Master's program, I gave some thought to pursuing a Ph.D., but though I eventually accumulated thirty additional graduate credits, I never seriously sought it. I justified this with the observation that I was more interested in high school teaching that called for broader diversity instead of further specialization that a doctorate demanded. The fear of failure, admittedly, was also a contributor to my decision.

5. CHARGES OF RADICALISM

"You are ignorant and foolish and as a teacher you are a danger to our youth. I will try to set you straight and will pray that you see the light for your sake and ours." These startling words came from an animated stranger in the Sunday evening audience at Lansdale Mennonite after I had given a talk on the topic "A Christian's Responsibility to His Government." Thus began my prolonged skirmish with a local Mennonite preacher, who, as a follower of Carl McIntyre, felt the essential part of his ministry was to defend the American economic and political systems. Since I was perceived to be a "dupe of the Communist conspiracy" he launched a personal inquisition determined to stamp out my heresy.

Soon after the initial confrontation, I accepted an invitation to visit him at his home. As I entered his library in a converted chicken house, the volume of resources he had accumulated amazed me. As he showed me copy after copy of printed pages of anti-communist propaganda, I was appalled by the twisted logic and vitriolic tirades presented in the name of Christianity. One diatribe went on to say that, "Communists are nothing more than rats, and like rats they should all be exterminated." When I questioned him as to how he could reconcile Anabaptist principles with his crusade, he simply said his ministry was a response to the Spirit's call. At that point, in a moment of rare feistiness, I asked him if he was sure he could distinguish between the voice of God and his own bull-headed ideas and walked out. Though we had no more such dramatic meetings, his efforts to set me straight persisted. I continued to receive periodicals and pamphlets dutifully delivered by his son, a student in one of my classes.

On another occasion the concern for my "soft stance" on Communism led to an evening interview with two local businessmen, one a fuel distributor and the other a member of the CD Board of Trustees. Principal Detweiler, who assured me that he had confidence in me and would support me as necessary, arranged the meeting on campus. Several months before the occasion, I had participated in a summer seminar on "Communism and Constitutional Democracy" at Westminster College in western Pennsylvania. Though the basic thrust was strongly anti-Communist to the core, the businessmen in seeing the title in a news release assumed it was of the opposite nature, and thus their interrogation.

I also had an encounter with John, a young man deeply involved in politics who had built a strong relationship with Mennonite youth in the Pennridge area. I had met him on a number of occasions as he visited on the CD campus, as well as meeting him occasionally at functions in the Perkasie Mennonite congregation. On one occasion, anticipating a good education, I had even gone with him to the Republican headquarters in Doylestown where local party leaders jovially watched the returns of the 1962 elections. At that point John did not know me as well as he thought he did. Then, on August 29, 1963 I received a lengthy letter from him. After quoting four Bible verses he went on to say

> Today I received a copy of the new voters registration for East Rockhill Township and find that the record for our district would have been perfect, except for the registration of one Democrat, whose name is listed as S. Duane Kauffman. However, from the standpoint of a personal rebuff, I am honestly not offended. . . . Ordinarily, I would regard a person's political views as none of my business, but, due to a very real

and genuine concern for the young people who are subject to the influence of these views and political doctrines, I feel completely justified in expressing my opinions to you.

He went on to relate how some CD students had been of the opinion that I had "Democratic leanings" but he had tried to convince them otherwise and that things I said were designed to "provoke thought and stimulate discussion." He then went on to say, "Now I wonder if I was correct in this position and feel that possibly I should apologize to these kids for challenging their conclusions, as your party registration speaks for itself and would seem to prove them more correct than I, in their opinions that your philosophy follows the 'Liberal-Democrat' line." The four single-spaced pages that followed were a well-designed plan to convince me that Republican Party positions were the only possible choices for enlightened Christians. A subsequent visit to the farm where he was boarding failed to close the wide gulf between us.

On Monday October 20, 1969 I found a letter from a local Mennonite pastor in my school mailbox. I was anticipating responses to an action I had taken the previous Wednesday, which across the land was hailed as Moratorium Day by those opposing the war in Vietnam. I had engaged Harley Kooker, a CD alumnus who had spent three years in voluntary service in Vietnam, to speak in my classes. I decided to go as far as to wear a black armband that day to identify with those calling for a cessation of United States military action. Somehow the word got out and a photographer caught it all in a picture published in the *North Penn Reporter*. The letter was written in a humble, thoughtful, and brotherly manner. He expressed disappointment in my conduct of the day as well as my statements made in classes that raised questions about the legitimacy of our military involvement in Southeast Asia. He went on to say that he felt Christians should refrain from criticizing the government and suggested that my best course of action would have been to call students together for a session of prayer for our political leaders.

There were other letters and occasions when I had to respond to those who were concerned about classroom incidents or the general direction in which they felt I was going. Responding by letter or in one-to-one conversations was not that difficult. The real challenge came when in a group context during parent-

1969 Presentation by Alumnus Harley Kooker.
Wearing black arm band as Vietnam War protest.

teacher's meetings I would be asked to articulate my Christian interpretation of history or to show how my teaching would differ from that presented in a public school setting. It usually seemed that those who raised the issue were laying a snare or were capitalizing on the moment to promote their own perspective that was often seen in absolute terms.

In my response I would say that it is my understanding that history is the unfolding of God's plans that will culminate at the end of time. I believe the hand of God is at work in history, but understanding this is beyond human comprehension. Therefore, I avoided implications that suggested that the small pox infestations, military conquest, and deportation were examples of Native American punishments for barbarism and spiritualism. Neither did I view the devastation of the South during the Civil War as God's affliction on them for their inhuman slavery, nor did I present the Great Depression as divine retribution for the immorality of the "Roaring Twenties."

The role of the historian is to attempt to tell the story as it really happened. The Christian teacher, when placing a premium on integrity, has a strong obligation to work extra hard to present a complete and accurate account. History is often abused because it is frequently postured in such a way that it supports a pre-determined position. Distortion does not come so much from presenting inaccurate details, but rather, by selecting and presenting the segments that lead to their anticipated conclusion.

From time to time I received criticism for departing from the traditional textbook story line or for exposing "saintly" American heroes as humans with feet of clay. As a Christian teacher I felt I should provide opportunities for students to read excerpts from Columbus' own journal as well as other contemporary writings so students could weigh the extreme possibilities of his being sent forth as "Christ Bearer" on the one hand, or on the other, one who was so greedy for gold he pursued a policy that came close to genocide. I provided material that showed the extraordinarily harsh treatment of conscientious Loyalists and Washington's lack of military leadership as evidenced by his inability to discipline foraging troops in our local community. Until recently revised textbook accounts were available, I had to find other sources so that students would even know about the "Galloway Plan," "Trail of Tears," World War II internment of Japanese-American citizens, or the extra cargo on the Lusitania.

Since history is perceived through human frames of reference, absolute objectivity is not possible. Admittedly I taught with an obvious Mennonite-Anabaptist bias. This did not mean that I deliberately tried to indoctrinate my students, but it did mean that I attempted to be sure that when wars and other issues were studied, alternate responses were examined and issues relating to human justice received maximum attention.

Was I a radical? Yes, but a moderate one. I "rocked the boat" at times with some strong personal feelings that developed into agendas that I attempted to carry out. Sometimes in the classroom I was deliberately controversial as a ploy to induce students to think. There were times when I challenged community standards on issues pertaining to financial priorities, racism, or dealing with criminal offenders. I was neither a Communist nor an advocate of communism, but I was soft on Communism in the sense that I did not feel that fighting it should become a Christian's major preoccupation. Did I get carried away at times? Yes! In retrospect, I am willing to admit that wearing the black armband in class was a questionable response. Then too, iconoclasm got in my blood, and at times I got carried away in stoning sacred cows.

Was I a liberal? Yes, I plead guilty to the charge, but I've always preferred to be thought of as a progressive. When I moved into the Bucks-Mont community I had no concept of how deeply entrenched local conservatism was. Since my grandfather and father were employed in the WPA, I naturally would choose Roosevelt's approach over Hoover's in terms of responding to the Great Depression. My advisor in graduate school worked on the Harold Ickes' New Deal team in the Department of Interior and influenced me to write my Master's dissertation on a comparative study of Progressive mayors "Golden Rule" Jones of Toledo and Tom L. Johnson of Cleveland. In addition to these influences, I am inclined to equate Anabaptist priorities on peace and justice with the philosophies of those in what is thought as being to the left.

As a teacher I tried not to show my liberal bent. Though I know it was strongly suspected, I never acknowledged my membership in the Democratic Party. I tried hard to respect those whose conservative views ran counter to mine, but it would be interesting to know if others feel I succeeded on that score.

6. THE REBELLIOUS HYPOCRITE

"Mr. Kauffman, the one thing I remember about you is that you made me get a haircut before I could go on chorus tour." This was the assertion of Cleon as he recalled his CD days forty years before. Today I am appalled when I consider the possibility that these kinds of bitter memories are common, and at times I wonder if I should not pay certain alumni a visit and apologize for such actions.

A primary motive for the founding of Christopher Dock Mennonite High School was to provide a means for dealing with the worldly pressures on the Mennonite youth of the 1950s and '60s. That being the case, the school's original "Constitution and Standards" set forth an impressive list of specific guidelines for students. The category receiving the greatest attention pertained to appearance. Though the code has changed from time to time to reflect prevailing church patterns, it has remained as a tempting barrier over which students are inclined to jump.

Dress standards for girls dealt with acceptable neckline, hemline, and sleeve lengths. No jewelry or cosmetics were allowed. Girls who were members of the Mennonite Church were required to wear the devotional covering, and arrange their hair in a way that accommodated it. From the beginning, detecting some infractions such as facial cosmetics made enforcement arbitrary or even unlikely.

Since dress requirements for boys called for minimum sacrifice, they usually pushed the limits with "extreme hairstyles."

Sometimes the issue centered on the length, while in other cases the styling was called into question. Strange as it may seem, the potentially offensive DA (Duck's Ass) was permitted, but a back neck trim that culminated with a straight line, subjected the student to a trip to the barber to have the offending "box cut's" stripe obliterated.

Enforcing policies for which I had no personal conviction, made me feel somewhat hypocritical. It would have been much easier to turn the other way, (Sometimes I did, such as not requiring girls to wear bonnets during their class trip), but I was part of a team that was commissioned to support the contemporary standards of the constituent churches.

My real hypocrisy lay in the fact that I asked students to submit to expectations in place for them, while I was unwilling to yield to those that were laid down for me. Something within me made me "step over the traces" from time to time. I tended to see the Board of Trustees and the Religious Welfare Committee as being behind the times and felt that some force was needed to bring necessary reform. Perhaps there were times when my intentions were less noble and I was simply "getting my kicks" by being "naughty."

A collarless plain coat had never been part of my wardrobe, but I had agreed to don one upon my employment at CD. Several days before the school year began Principal Detweiler took me to Souders' to have my regular coat made into a "straight cut." He had previously confided that the plain coat issue was in transition and it would probably work out if I chose to wear it only for school functions. Though the cost of the alteration was minimal, I still did not get my money's worth because I only wore it on two occasions: the first parent-teacher's meeting and the day pictures were taken for the school yearbook. I never wore a coat and tie combination in class, but taught coatless, sometimes wearing a tie and in other cases, a regular sport shirt. My insubordination was somewhat diminished since I was merely following the lead of Ben Hess, a respected charter member of the faculty. During my second year, Hess, Hiram Hershey, newcomer Roy Hartzler and I wore regular coat and tie combinations in violation of policy. During exchanges with the Board and Religious Welfare Committee each of us strongly intimated that we would not return if the matter were pushed. Before my third year began, the issue had been resolved. The requirement was dropped after returned questionnaires from the school constituents showed little support for the plain coat regulation.

Another rule where I chose to test the limits was the jewelry provision that banned wedding rings. Though not a part of our wedding ceremony, Naomi and I felt wedding bands would not only be an appropriate expression of our mutual love, but also provide a public manifestation of our marital status. As a stand against ostentation, we made white gold our choice. I dutifully removed it for school occasions, but for sports events and public programs I sometimes "forgot" to take it off. After several notes and an eventual interview with the principal I agreed to be more discreet. At that point, Principal Yoder took the issue to the Board of Trustees and after considerable time and debate the wedding ring was exempted from the jewelry policy.

Though the Board or Administration never confronted me for my "flat top," a reading of board minutes showed it was a constant concern. Things took an interesting turn when I succumbed to Beatle mania and returned from my sabbatical in Britain with long hair and sideburns. When that change found general acceptance I was emboldened to grow a beard, albeit in the modified mustacheless Lincoln mode. After a year I relinquished it since, as a baseball coach I felt obligated to model the "No facial hair policy" required of the players. For various reasons after one year, I left coaching and decided to go all the way —mustache and all. Lo and behold, other faculty members followed suit and today a male CD teacher without facial hair of some sort is in a stark minority. My hairy expression was a demonstration of sympathy for those protesting the status quo.

In my case I have retained the look because I like it and I have become too conservative to change.

My recent retirement house cleaning included going through my files to determine what to keep and what should be tossed. In doing this I uncovered some long-forgotten documents I had composed and released. They were quite comprehensive and gave evidence of considerable thought. For much of the material I am proud to claim ownership, but for some, I am horrified by my presumptuousness, and in some cases, lack of perspective. Two of my more memorable treatises pertaining to grading and campus design are included in the *Appendix*. A summary of five others follows.

On October 5, 1969 I made a presentation in a parent-teacher's meeting in which I attempted to show that the low percentage of students on the honor roll could be attributed to student employment and access to cars. After making the observation that, "Students need to work to pay off and maintain the car which is needed to get to work," I concluded by asking the question, "Is the car worth the inferior achievement it may bring in school, or the premature independence your son or daughter gains?"

In April 1971, after the Board of Trustees had decided to freeze teacher salaries, I sent the board a letter along with my unsigned contract for the following year. After making six points criticizing the decision I gave four recommendations. One was the creation of a salary and benefits committee with faculty representation. This particular suggestion was implemented the following year.

In the same year I submitted a "Counter Proposal for Student Government" which would have created five commissions with the "chief commissioner of each making up the presidium (note the radical term) which would coordinate commission activities, determine areas of responsibility, and provide overall direction." This recommendation did not receive serious consideration.

In 1972 I sent a written response to the Board of Trustees after they decided our school would join the Suburban Athletic League. My six reasons maintained that the faculty position was not taken seriously, a good intramural program would serve our purposes better, there would be the possibility of greater vandalism and crowd control problems, the traveling distances were excessive, the gym and public conveniences were inadequate, and our school would be outclassed by teams in the higher brackets.

In the spring of 1975 I proposed that "an afternoon be spent by the returning faculty and those recently elected to the staff as a time of functioning as a Christian community for the purpose of discerning and affirming each other's gifts, culminating in the filling of extra-curricular tasks for which faculty members will be responsible during the coming school year." Though the plan was dismissed as being too idealistic, the responsibility for filling co-curricular positions was given to a committee that included three faculty representatives.

My last major epistle was a May 1994 document entitled "Graduation of Marginal Students." My major concern was the practice of "allowing some who came up short on academic requirements to walk across the platform and shake hands with a member of the Board and receive what was perceived to be a diploma." I pointed out that this practice lacked integrity, was unfair to faculty and other students, and encouraged indolence and irresponsibility.

In this review it seems like I played the role of a gadfly and perhaps at times I even made myself obnoxious. Maybe I was motivated somewhat by the thrill of stirring things up. Though not taking exclusive credit, I feel good about the many suggestions I made that set things in motion which have helped to make CD what it has become.

7. SETTING THE TONE

"Plays the role of professor well," "Let's get organized," "Unique style of lectures," "Interesting illustrations," "Maintains class discipline," "Dislikes people sleeping in class." This sampling of captions under my 1962, 1963, and 1964 school yearbook photos already projected an image that would not differ much from what students would perceive forty years later.

After early years of learning by trial and error and the development of greater competency, I developed a teaching style that placed a premium on captainship. Along the way a persona developed that took on a life of its own.

A major turning point in my career occurred after I learned more about myself and decided to play the personal cards I had been dealt. One that often served as trump was my voice. In time I recognized its proper utilization enabled me to create a commanding presence. Some even said it reminded them of God. Along the way I learned to capitalize on my individuality, even manipulating my idiosyncrasies to my best advantage.

Zeus had his bolt of lightning, Odysseus his trusty bow, King Arthur his gigantic sword, and many myths have emerged on the theme of Kauffman's omnipresent yardstick. Though its initial use was to serve as a pointer, it eventually became a convenient symbol of authority. It provided effective reinforcement and at times was displayed in a menacing manner, but many rumors about its application are absolutely false. Though student assertions that they felt the air might well be true, and though I admit

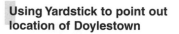
Using Yardstick to point out
location of Doylestown

to using it to bang on desks and waste cans, I honestly and adamantly insist that I never hit a student with it. Today the artifact is in two pieces waiting for its placement in some appropriate museum. Under my use it developed splinters and cracks but its permanent division occurred while I was on sabbatical leave. Let it also be said that during the second half of my teaching career I functioned very well without it.

For me a cardinal principle to be followed was to be in control at all times. I found one of the keys to successful classroom management was to foster a sense of expectancy. Generating momentum after arriving late to class was very difficult. Therefore, even if it required a cross-campus sprint, I made it a top priority to be in the classroom before the tardy bell rang. I tried to start the class with a sense of urgency. This might take the form of a quiz on their desk when they arrived, a bell-ringer question, or a quick review of the previous day's lesson.

Articulating well-defined behavioral expectations and providing consistent enforcement were also very important. I did not follow Dr. Wong's precept of posting a list of rules on the classroom wall because to me it was too much "in your face" and beneath the dignity of high school adolescents. Students soon learned who was in charge, and that disrespect for classmates and me, or a disruption in the flow of the moment would not be tolerated.

In my early teaching days I occasionally sent students to the principal's office for correction. However, I became a firm believer in the necessity of a teacher taking responsibility for his or her discipline problems. In a few emergencies I simply dismissed students from the room. At times I re-arranged seating or set up a noontime or after-school conference. In some cases I dealt with the situation on the spot. Sometimes the activity was temporarily stopped and a stern stare ensued while at other times a few reminders were given, but on other occasions my response took on the form of a sarcastic censure.

During the first class period of a new quarter, in order to create a serious impression and to aid in long range planning, I distributed materials that carefully outlined academic requirements. This included a schedule of daily lesson topics with accompanying reading assignments and a description of homework assignments and their due dates. Though some students were overwhelmed at the time, and some of the papers were lost, the organization and projection of the big picture were generally appreciated by the parents and students.

I have become strongly convinced that a good physical setting is necessary for teaching and learning. If firm classroom control is desired, considerable attention must be given to the seating scheme. After years of arranging my desks in the traditional checkerboard pattern I switched to a grouping of two rows placed in a large semicircle. Having the students face each other

With Drew Foderaro and James
Hanson in 2001 Classroom

did wonders for group dynamics. Despite the temptation to take advantage of the neighboring student's close proximity, I found control easier since I could get closer to each student without having my back turned.

After my first year I realized that one of my major problems in classroom management was the fact that when given a chance, students would sit next to those with whom they were likely to chat or fool around. For a number of years I arranged the seating pattern alphabetically. This was an improvement over the old choose-your-own system and it facilitated collecting papers in grade book sequence. Problems still existed since familiar Moyer cousins sitting next to each other and the Landises close to their own kin, often yielded to the temptation of chitchat. Finally I settled on a plan in which I deliberately tried to provide a mix with quiet buffers next to the potentially disruptive ones. For grades nine and ten it worked quite well to use a simple boy then girl arrangement. By the time they were juniors and seniors this scheme had minimal effect. Fortunately by that time I had a good read on their disposition and arranged seating accordingly.

Throughout my teaching career I found myself in a variety of classroom settings. I am convinced that in addition to seating plans, other environmental factors also affect student and teacher performance. I found it extremely hard to be positive when over-crowded conditions, inadequate ventilation, dim lighting, and wretched temperatures took their physical and psychological toll. I have also discovered that good bulletin boards, posters, and pictures not only serve as good teaching tools, but also demonstrate the level of a teacher's commitment. In my case I reaped the benefit of a wife with bulletin board materials and skills even if she was often disappointed with the infrequency of removal and replacement. For over thirty years a major component of my classroom décor was my set of Presidents' portraits displayed in the front of my classroom. They provided a good study of the evolution of male fashions for the wandering minds and gave me a boost as a "great cloud of witnesses." Most important, they served as convenient pegs that helped to hold the chronological segments of American history together.

If an appealing classroom is important, a strong case can be made for the teacher to be tastefully attired. Convinced wearing a tie was indispensable in projecting a professional appearance, I doggedly continued the miserable practice even though most of my male colleagues had surrendered to comfortable informality

Though I eventually adopted a style that worked for me, I do not propose it as a model for others. It was not without flaws and many teachers reach their goals with a system that is as far removed from mine, as night is from day. Though my authoritative approach was affirmed by many students, albeit years after the fact, I am humbled when I realize some would have done better in a low-keyed, less structured setting.

8. ADDING SPICE

Good classroom management goes beyond conditioning behavior by imposing punishment for broken rules. Rather, the key to good discipline is to provide a setting in which the student is not inclined to misbehave. Classroom experiences must be interesting and worthwhile. The typical teenager at two o'clock in the afternoon can hardly be expected to sit attentively through forty minutes of a dull prescribed routine. A conscious effort must be made to provide changes of pace with a variety of meaningful activities and sufficient spice must be added to make the diet more palatable.

Though my reputation as a disciplinarian persisted, I received constant feedback from parents who told how their son or daughter gleefully regaled them at dinner with tales of Kauffman shenanigans in class that day. Five years ago CD alumnus Jeff, a law school student, spent several weeks observing and participating in my Criminal Justice class. After a class period, when my portrayal of the infamous Babbitt Case caused so much uproar, I had to close the door for the sake of other classes he said, "That was better strand-up comedy than what people pay to see in Atlantic City."

I have known very few excellent teachers who did not have a good sense of humor and use it to their full advantage. Humor comes in many forms. I have great difficulty in analyzing or comprehending my own style. It might seem that I was some kind of paradoxical combination of Sergeant Carter and Gomer Pyle.

The Gomer comparison bothers me because I am uneasy with the label of silly or even funny. I certainly did not want to cultivate a reputation as a clown or a buffoon.

In my case, my humor seemed to grow out of my manner of presentation, rather than a calculated sprinkling of puns or recycled *Readers' Digest* tidbits. Since humor can be found in almost anything, the trick is to find the light side or odd incongruity and present it in such a way that "truth will appear stranger than fiction." Though I never deliberately used him as a model, I would be pleased to be seen as a Will Rogers instead of a Gomer Pyle.

Good humor must not be seen as something canned, but rather as a spontaneous response to a particular situation. For me, at times, it meant a quick comeback to what somebody had just done or said. One example, in my case, grew out of the occasional male embarrassment of the unzipped fly. Usually a student's concern came in a hushed discreet whisper, but on one occasion in the middle of the class activity, a girl raised her hand and blurted, "Mr. Kauffman, your fly is open!" My quick retort was, "Well if you think you have seen something, your imagination is much better than your eyesight!"

On one occasion I noticed Fred in the back row catching a fly and then proceeding to torture it by dragging it over his book by a long hair he had tied around its head. Many years later Fred said, "He figured out a way to embarrass me without missing a beat in his lecture. In his deepest, loudest voice, mid lecture—as if it were just to emphasize a key point—he boomed out for all to hear, 'and the white man persecuted the Indian, the same way the man in the back is persecuting that fly right now.'"

I did seem to get the most mileage when the anecdotes were a teensy-weensy bit risqué. My Ancient Greece and Rome students will long remember details about the cosmetic application of Cretan women, the ithyphallic pranks of Alcibiades, or the banned hold in the Olympic pancration event.

The key to successful humor is to make it appear natural and spontaneous, but in all honesty, it often was something I had carefully programmed. At times I saw myself as an actor on the stage manipulating the audience with carefully calculated moves. Sometimes I repeated successful routines in one section of the class in the other ones later that day. In those cases I was often deflated when the flat responses indicated the plot had been divulged before its scheduled moment.

My students of the last thirty years have long forgotten the identity of many historical figures, but the name Beulah will bring a sparkle to the eye and a smile of recognition. Beulah was the mysterious colorful character that I often wove into my classroom narrative. In the speculation about her true identity, it was often rumored that she was my mother. In a May 2003 chapel presentation I publicly denied that, and revealed Gertrude to be my mother's name. This disclosure drew so many laughs that I had to wonder if my fictional character had been given the wrong name. No, Beulah was just a nice old-fashioned name that seemed to give my subject the right touch.

Though humor adds an essential spice to teaching, there are other ingredients that provide additional zest. Successful teachers find ways to enhance learning with field trips, guest resource persons, effective use of technology, bulletin boards, and stimulating posters. Spicing things up calls for creativity and sometimes requires extra effort and moving beyond one's comfort zone. As an added feature in my Civil War unit I brought my guitar to class and sang a collection of Civil War songs. Years before, I had done a similar thing in Criminal Justice when I presented a set of ballads about prison life. Not only did this provide an excellent way to supplement course content, it also allowed students to see me in a different light.

The Christopher Dock school year traditionally began with an evening event when new students, parents, faculty, and administration meet for an orientation for the coming year. Frequently a current student, often the Campus Senate president, addressed

Singing Civil War Songs
Left to right: Jonathan Moyer,
Jonas Yoder, Duane Kauffman

the in-coming students and in the context of things to expect, warned, "and don't fall asleep in Mr. Kauffman's class!" In meeting alumni, the stories about my methods of keeping students awake tops all the memories they wish to discuss. It would seem that if I would ever make the Pedagogical Hall of Fame, the first thing on my plaque would be an account of my wide assortment of sleep disturbing exploits.

Upon the realization that my actions had taken on such legendary proportions, I was motivated to try even harder to live up to my reputation. The last thing I wanted was to hear a student boasting of sleeping in Kauffman's class.

Along the way I did a considerable amount of throwing chalk and felt erasers. They were low velocity, high arching lobs, and though many alumni claim the honor of being hit, none was ever even slightly wounded in the assault. Sometimes I merely used my voice that by some accounts was capable of even waking the dead. Once I shouted to a dozing Bucks County farm boy, "Dan, get up it is time to milk the cows!" In another case involving Gerald an avid fisherman, I exclaimed, "Wake up you've got a bite!"

It was in keeping students awake that I found my greatest use for the yardstick. The early waste cans were metal and those in my room became quite dented. When I beat them with my yardstick they would sound like a ringing Chinese gong. Slapping it on the student's desk not only awoke the culprit in question but also shook up the whole class. I remember two mishaps resulting from hitting the table in the front of the room. Once I inadvertently broke two of my "Pilot Fine" ballpoint pens. Another time led to a serious consequence when an innocent girl in the front row lost control of her bladder and deposited a considerable volume of water on her seat.

A persisting story pertained to the time I sent sleepy Abe out to the mailbox on Forty Foot Road and since I didn't even give him a chance to get his coat I caused him to miss a week of school due to pneumonia. I was greatly relieved when Abe recently set the story straight. His absence was not due to pneumonia, but an ear infection instead. On a number of occasions I sent nodding students to the stop sign with a strip of masking tape giving them five or six minutes to make the O into a Q or the P into an R. Once I sent Mark outside the building to get a handful of snow and when he returned I made him rub it on his face. On two occasions I used the liquid contents of my teapot: once in baptizing Chris and perhaps in the boldest maneuver of all, tossing the contents into the lap of unsuspecting Andy.

Many of the students in question denied they were actually sleeping. One particular incident stands out. One of the Pottstown or Chester County Miller boys had fallen asleep in my last period class and didn't hear the final bell. After about five minutes I recognized the situation and knowing he did not come on the bus, I decided to let him sleep. After a half hour, I went back and shook him only to hear him say, "I wasn't sleeping I was just resting my eyes!"

My sleep waking efforts were intended to deal with individual offenders. Yet, they were often staged for maximum classroom effect. Perhaps, to a certain extent, my dramatic gestures grew out of the assumption that I was a failure since my efforts were not good enough to sustain sufficient interest. Hopefully it might also be said that the same students dozed off in other classes and the real reason was a simple case of insufficient sleep the night before.

9. THE DRILLMASTER IS A TEDDY BEAR

"When I was in Mr. Kauffman's class for the first time I was scared to death, but once I got to know him, he became a close friend and one of my favorite teachers." These were the words frequently heard during the culminating senior presentations. It would seem that in my case "what you saw" was not necessarily "what you got." Apparently much of my external expression belied my real nature.

If I were judged solely on my style in classroom management and instructional techniques, some observers would most certainly conclude that I was in the wrong institution and I should have been on the receiving, rather than the giving end. However, there was a third more intangible dimension working for me and that was my relationship with my students. It was this rapport that gave me license to do the unorthodox things for which I was known.

One of a teacher's highest callings is to be an encourager. Colonial schoolmaster Christopher Dock was noted for the love he had for his pupils. Since Dock felt his ability to love was a gift from God, he constantly looked for ways to show it. One of his most frequent expressions of love was to affirm students with a kind word or a prized artifact as a tangible reward. In this respect I have tried to emulate Dock as a teacher and in doing so I have seen that appropriate gestures often stimulate growth from a state of dormancy to an eventual array of spectacular bloom.

The encouraged are more likely to pass it on and become encouragers. In my college experience it was a timely validation by an English professor that produced a significant turning point. In my sophomore year I found myself enrolled in Literature Interpretation. At that point I lacked confidence and interpreting literature, prose or poetry, was not one of my interests. One of the major course assignments was to choose a noted person as a subject and present a biographical radio address. After other students had selected names of religious, political, and literary figures, I announced my preference as "Babe" Ruth. As several in the classroom tittered, Brother Pellman hesitated, but gave no sign of disapproval. As a baseball fan, I had a special interest in the subject. This spurred me to a high level of effort, which even saw me walk into town to use the public library's resources. When the big day came I was the last of four to give our addresses. When I was finished Professor Pellman said, "Now that is the way to give a radio address!" He gave me a good mark for its literary quality and selected me as one of four in the class to actually give the speech on WEMC. Before the course was over I was volunteering to read poetry, receiving considerable praise for my dramatic presentations of Blake's "The Tiger" and Sandburg's "Chicago."

The way a teacher responds to student classroom input has far-reaching implications. The teacher's positive response may inspire the student to strive for greater things. On the other hand, the teacher's lack of approval may not only stifle potential productivity, but also be taken as a put-down with serious emotional ramifications. Though in lighter situations I may have called a student's banter a "bunch of cockamamie," I made it a point to accept and build on student comments even if it meant putting a positive spin on what was often pretty far "off the wall."

Years ago, Lowell, a pastor in one of the local congregations said, "I disliked school and was bored in your class. I sat in the back and never said anything. One time I did and you said, 'That is a good perspective.'" From that time on, I got involved in more discussions and ended up liking the class and getting a decent grade. That gave me the push that helped me to get to where I am now."

Bev had been out of school for several days as a result of injuries sustained in a car accident. When she arrived in my class and approached my desk I was shocked by her swollen face and black eye. I tried not to show it and walked over to her, put my arm around her and said, "Bev you still look beautiful to me!" Today she says, "That was exactly what I needed."

Taking my clue from Schoolmaster Dock and remembering its importance to me, I made it a practice to strike up conversations with students during which I would give them a compliment of some kind. Perhaps it was for some achievement, or it might have been a comment on how they looked. I was always amazed at how that overture opened the door for significant exchanges later.

As it happened, there were a few students with whom I had a closer bond. In some cases it came with the territory of being their assigned advisor. As I walked beside class officers or Campus Senate presidents giving them support and reassurance, it was very satisfying to see them develop leadership skills and self-confidence.

There were some almost inexplicable cases where I found myself assuming a role that could be described as primary care-giver. There were a few students, male and female, that seemed to latch onto me, spending as much time with me as possible. For these students I became a confidant and throughout the years at least a half-dozen said they wished I were their father.

These relationships were very taxing in terms of energy and time. It frequently raised the issue of priorities because some-times they were there before and after school and occasionally part of the noon period as well, which did not allow much time for other necessary details such as last-minute preparation for classes. With these intense relationships came a heavy responsi-bility that called for superhuman astuteness. At times I felt caught in the middle as the recipient of confidential information that seemed serious enough to call for intervention beyond my sphere. Though at times this involvement presented challenges in maintaining professional distance, I found these especially close relationships to be extremely rewarding. It was deeply gratifying to know I was helping to meet a need in the student's life and the friendship was mutually fulfilling.

As a cheerleader and quality field hockey player, vivacious Amy was popular and seemed to have it all together. Yet I sensed shallowness and an unwillingness to strive for excellence. We had developed a good relationship built partly around her strong commitment to feminism. We engaged in considerable kidding, both in class and out, as I questioned her assertion that cheerleading should be considered a sport and teased her about the expectation that I would change my name from Kauffman to "Kauffperson." One day after a class in U.S. Government, in which she failed to display knowledge of basic details, I detained her and said, "Amy, do you really not know this, or are you just pulling my leg? Years later Amy would say, "I remember giving you excuses for my poor performance and you wouldn't accept any of them. You believed in me, which meant more than you know. Your laughter, booming voice, and words of encouragement will always be with me."

When time came at the end of the junior year for students to volunteer to run for senior class president I urged her to run for the office. After considerable convincing she did and was elected by her classmates and did a commendable job. At my retirement reception she offered the following words:

> One of my most amusing memories of Mr. Kauffman happened on one of my first days of school my senior year. The freshmen were all sitting against the lockers in Dielman Hall, as first-years do, talking amongst themselves. I came bounding down the hallway and gave Mr. Kauffman a giant hug. I remember the look on those freshmen faces was one of utter amazement. It was though Goliath himself reached down and gave David a hug. You see, Mr. Kauffman is much

1996 Commencement, with Amy
Moore and Julianna Clemmer

like an urban legend among first-years. The cup of water poured on a student's lap became a bucket, the chalk that was tossed, was thrown, and the tapping on a student's desk became a slam of the ruler. And like most urban legends, no one ever knows the entire truth.

Bubbly Heather was academically motivated and had special interests and abilities in music but her bipolar disorder brought on long bouts of incapacitating depression leaving her with feelings of hopelessness and vulnerability. There were times when she looked to me as a person to see her through. Lacking professional expertise and feeling inadequate, I saw my role as listening and letting her know that I cared. Occasionally I made a special trip to see her on her job. I also encouraged her to take advantage of a summer opportunity to be part of a mission's choir tour to Europe that turned out to be a highlight in her life. At my retirement reception she came to the microphone and thanked me profusely for standing beside her along the way. I was touched and humbled when among other comments she said, "I wanted to give up on myself, but you wouldn't let me. You always gave me a hug and you never gave up on me. You saw me as God saw me and you believed in me."

10. BEYOND THE CLASSROOM

If I was under the impression that the role of a teacher was confined to the classroom, that illusion vanished quickly. I soon found myself involved in activities known then as extra-curricular, but today as co-curricular. There were numerous times when these assignments took more time and created more stress than classroom instruction. They presented challenges that helped to cultivate resourcefulness and flexibility. They also provided good opportunities to develop relationships with students as I interacted with them in a more informal setting.

During my first six years I was the faculty advisor for Student Council. This was a formal institution and I had to quickly master *Robert's Rules of Order*. In addition to serving as parliamentarian I worked with the Executive Committee that was responsible for creating the agenda and seeing that decisions were carried out.

In 1970 I found myself on the Traffic and Safety Committee that dealt primarily with parking and speeding violations. In that same year I was involved in a major reorganization that created a body known as the Campus Senate. The four (later decreased to three) members of the faculty were not called advisors but senators just like the students who were elected to serve. The new structure was designed to create an impression of faculty-student cooperation on equal terms. The new concept was put to a quick test when under the aggressive leadership of President Ehst, the faculty senators were outvoted and measures were passed eliminating detention hall and installing a candy vending machine.

1997 Campus Senate
First Row, Left to right: Nelson Martin, Lisa Kegg, Melissa Rice, Regan Derstine, Amanda Fenchel, Amy Geissinger, David Brewer, Kathryn Hunsberger. Second Row: Duane Kauffman, David Guengerich, Angela Ehst, Christina Anastasi, Andrew Martin, Jonathan Paine, Leah Reiff

On a number of occasions I served as the faculty member on the School Activities Committee and found that assignment to be extremely demanding. This body was responsible to plan and orchestrate all-school socials. Though students went ahead with these tasks, two others called for more individual initiative. One of these was to assume responsibility for school assemblies by securing and hosting the guest presenter and introducing him or her to the student audience. The occasion that really put me to the test was Spring Arts Day. It was my responsibility to secure judges, determine the schedule, provide a printed program, present an introduction and devotional that set the tone, in addition to facilitating the specific competition events. It also entailed selecting the components and serving as master of ceremonies for the public program that took place the following evening. Finally, one of the most challenging features was to find the best way to announce the competition results.

One of the rewards for Student Council and Campus senators was the opportunity to be part of the annual retreat at Mininger's Cabin, Men-O-Lan, Spruce Lake, Lake Wallenpaupeck, or the Blue Mountain Retreat Center. In the early years the outing consisted of the entire Student Council. Later it became a leadership retreat that involved not only the Campus Senate Executive Committee but also class officers, team captains, and publication editors as well. The occasion provided opportunities for informal mingling during recreational activities and picnics. It was also a time of stimulating group discussions and responding to the input of guest resource persons. For me, the highlight was the spiritual enrichment provided by student-led worship and times of sharing stories of personal journeys.

From the beginning of the school's history, one of the extra-curricular options was to participate in clubs that met during the scheduled activities period. In the early 1960s I sponsored a Pen Pals Club in which members, using names supplied by a clearing house, corresponded with foreign students who were interested in improving their English language skills. Another short-lived club in which I was involved, was the Folk Music Club. We did some singing to guitar accompaniment, but most of the time was spent in listening to 60s folk as well as recordings of folk songs from other lands. The year's highlight was a trip to the Academy of Music in Philadelphia to hear Peter, Paul, and Mary. As the advisor I experienced considerable chagrin when I was informed the next day that we had left Eddie stranded in Philadelphia and his parents had to go down after him in the wee hours of the morning.

For seven years the Numismatics Club flourished in the late 1960s and early 1970s. For several years it was the largest and most active club on campus. We took trips to the U.S. Mint and the Franklin Mint in Philadelphia, but most of our time was spent sorting through coins to fill Whitman folders or to find those with auction value. Club members bought shares of stock

1967 Numismatics Club
Clockwise: Aaron Kolb, Dale Yoder, Allen Yoder, Ralph Hedrick, Duane Kauffman, Daniel Walters, (unidentified), Darrel Hostetter, Steve Hackman

in the club and the money raised was used to buy bags of coins, usually from the West Coast, since they provided many with an S mintmark. These goodies were then auctioned to the highest bidder with club profits distributed in proportion to the purchased shares of stock.

Though intensely interested in sports, my athletic involvement at CD was minimal. During the early years I directed and officiated intramural activities. I also did some commentary for basketball videotaping. My only coaching experience came in 1972 when, with Al Martin, we launched our school's interscholastic baseball program. Due to circumstances beyond our control we were forced to begin our schedule without uniforms or our own playing field. As the season progressed, playing in new uniforms on their own well-manicured diamond, the multi-talented, highly motivated team won the Keystone Conference Eastern Division crown with a record of ten wins and only one defeat. Then in a day to remember, thanks to Tom's outstanding pitching and timely three-run homer, the Pioneers defeated Patton, the representative from the Western Division, and came away with a huge championship trophy.

Though rampant recidivism raised questions about effectiveness, detention was used as a convenient way of dealing with common misdemeanors and tardiness to class. In earlier years the teacher who challenged the behavior usually implemented his or her own plan. Eventually, a system was initiated which provided a twenty-minute "time-out" during the lunch period. For the last twelve years it was my lot to supervise this group activity. In truth, I volunteered for the task since it exempted me from other supervisory obligations and allowed me to stay in my own classroom.

For awhile students were required to complete a form on which they described the nature of the offense, indicated a willingness to work at improvement, and if answered in the affirmative, present a specific plan for remediation. The formality was finally dropped when its value was deemed worthless. (I was amused on several occasions when a student's true attitude was inadvertently divulged, when instead of writing, "definitely yes" the student gave the misspelled version of "defiantly yes.")

Detention was not much of a hardship. Talking and sleeping were banned and students were confined to a particular desk. Most of the students simply used the opportunity to do homework though a few merely sat and meditated or gazed at Presidents' portraits. At times I engaged a students in low-keyed conversation if the circumstances were right. It might have been an opportunity to let them vent, or perhaps it was an effort to encourage them to engage in some serious introspection.

Lynn was a typical student who lacked sufficient motivation. I was impressed by her insights and ability to express herself in my classes. Along the way I tried to challenge her to greater heights, going as far as urging her to consider a career in law. I never seemed to reach her and was pleasantly surprised when during her senior presentation she expounded on how much she had benefited from our conversations during detention.

Of all the roles beyond the classroom, the responsibilities of the class advisor were the most encompassing. This was especially true in the early days when two co-advisors alone were in charge of the wide range of activities.

Until the early 1960s each grade had its annual class trip. In May of 1959, during my first school year, Mr. Clemens and I accompanied the ninth graders to the state capital in Harrisburg. On the way we stopped at the ironworks at Hopewell Village. The highlight was on our return when we enjoyed a stomach-stuffing family style dinner around the big tables at the Shartlesville Hotel.

The following year it was New York City. Here we took in attractions such as the Statue of Liberty, United Nations Headquarters, and Empire State Building. We had lunch in an automat and dinner in Chinatown. My most vivid memory was the awesome burden thrust upon me when my co-advisor Stanley Shenk deserted us by going to Union Theological Seminary for the weekend finding his own way home. I also remember the bus ride home when I had to endure the humiliation of Jim's play-by-play rendition of Branca's "gopher ball" in the 1951 play-off. The junior class trip was to Washington, D.C. My memories of that experience are crowded out by later Senior class occasions there, but one that lingers was the annoying fifteen minute wait on the bus at Mount Vernon until a student, now a local cardiologist, came nonchalantly strolling into view.

The senior trip was a three-day tour of parts of Virginia where our two-night stay in Williamsburg included side excursions to Yorktown and Jamestown. On the return, stops were made at Monticello, Natural Bridge, and Luray Caverns. Four years later during the senior trip to Washington, D.C. a frustrating occasion arose that called for an impromptu decision to change motels after arrival. We had booked a Howard Johnson motel in Alexandria and students were eagerly anticipating using the swimming pool advertised in the publicity brochure. When we arrived to check in, we were informed the pool was closed for repairs. At that point, with the cooperation of the motel chain and the bus driver, we chose to go to another Howard Johnson's in Cheverly on the other side of the city. The hastily arranged rooming scheme put the boys and girls on the same floor but their gratitude for the extra consideration seemed to put them in a cooperating mood.

Another important senior event was the weekend retreat at Camp Swatara in Lebanon County. This was a great time of fun, food, and fellowship and the opportunity was taken for us to "let our hair down" and engage in some things forbidden on campus such as singing with piano and guitar accompaniment and viewing the spectacular *Third Man on the Mountain*. I had my hands full dealing with lively boys who swam fully clothed in the off-limits pond, gave the girls a midnight whistle serenading, and stoned a poor raccoon to death. Unfortunately, my most vivid memory was the black eye, throbbing headache, and ringing ears as a result of colliding with a tree when I went out for a long pass thrown by quarterback Nyce.

Diagramming a Play, 1962
Left to right: Jim Halteman, Noah Kolb,
Herb Myers, Vernon Nyce, Victor Myers

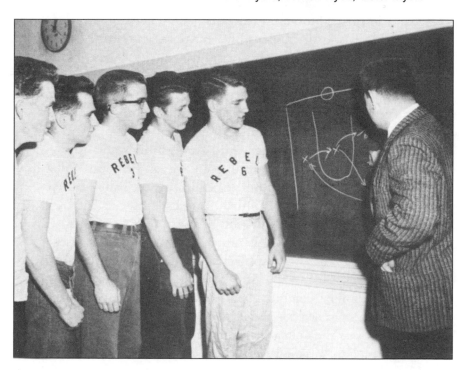

In my first year, I was an advisor for the ninth grade class and remained with them until they graduated in 1962. In addition to class trips, I coached the "Rebels" in basketball and softball as well as track and field events for Spring Day. Due to my coaching ineptitude and limited talent pool, our losses seemed to exceed our victories. Yet I was left with fond memories of Noah's soft left-handed jump shot, Vic's blinding speed, Harry's hustle, Herb's odd-looking eyeglasses guard, Vernie's shot-put toss, and "Fatty's" chatter and catcher's mitt he wore on his right hand.

In the days of smaller class sizes students were assigned to a homeroom. In this setting the homeroom teacher took care of details such as taking attendance, making announcements and supervising study during activities period for students not enrolled in clubs. On Thursdays, instead of attending the regular chapel in the auditorium, each class had homeroom devotions. Though this was the responsibility of the class officers I often found myself frustrated as I engaged in some hectic last minute improvisation.

Another significant expectation of class advisors was to coach the events of Spring Forensics, later called Spring Arts Day. Though music, literature, and drama were not my areas of expertise, I enjoyed working with students in vocals, poetry, readings, and plays. Today I still see Lester as "Wildcat Willie" and Rick as the handler of the graceful Lee Mee. I still hear Joel doing "What it was, was Football," Steve's "Casey at Bat," and the widely acclaimed presentation of Poe's "Bells" by Chrissie. I also will not forget the Sue's masterfully rendered "The Life of Lincoln West" that was unexpectedly and inexplicably spurned by the judges.

Early Junior-Senior Banquets were more involved because they not only called for the lavishly decorated setting and the meal, but also the drama that followed. The one that I remember most fondly was the 1961 production of "Little Women" performed in New England setting. It was especially meaningful because it was a project in which my wife and I collaborated. I also remember the innovative arrangement of building tiers upon which the banquet tables were placed while the performance took place on the floor below.

In the mid 1970s the class advisor concept was redefined. Each member of the faculty was assigned from 12 to 16 students in a particular class. The teachers with advisor groups from the same class functioned as a team with a chief advisor designated to systematize class activities. The advisor group arrangement was seen as an opportunity for faculty members to relate more closely to a specific body of students with the hope that a group identity would develop. In reality, because of schedule restraints,

2003 Junior-Senior Banquet
With Loriane Bundu (left) and Allandria Edwards (right)

the role of the class advisor took on a more routine posture of supervising study and chapel behavior as well as helping with course registration and grade card distribution. In the new plan the team of advisors in that particular grade shared Arts Day and Junior-Senior Banquet and senior end-of-year activities. Class trips to Washington and later to the winter retreat in Connecticut were less demanding since major planning and execution were in the hands of an appointed coordinator. Though the advisor group plan never reached its full potential, it was not a failure. I invited several of my groups to our home and we had a good time together. I also liked the practice of having the advisors write a letter of welcome and challenge to their assignees at the beginning of the new school year. Occasionally there were also opportunities for the group to discuss chapels or other themes that were very profitable.

II. A MENTOR AND SUPERVISING TEACHER

It is one thing to advise and instruct students, but something different to be called upon to assist those preparing to teach and those who are taking their first steps in the profession. During my years at CD I served as a mentor for three beginning teachers and on five occasions as a supervisor of student teachers. Though I was honored that my administrators saw me as a master teacher and entrusted me with the responsibility, I am humbled when I reflect on the level of my commitment and the quality of my performance.

In these roles I tended to take a "hands-off" approach. As they "learned by doing" I tried to be available to listen and encourage, sharing some of the "tricks of the trade" that I had picked up along the way. My reluctance to take a more dynamic course reflected my own feelings of inadequacy, but also grew out of an awareness that ultimately one learns to teach from the stern master of experience.

As mentor for Sam and Monty I was part of a state mandated program that provided guidelines to be followed and required the maintaining and submission of detailed records. In both cases we came up short in meeting all the expectations and only some last-minute attention salvaged the opportunity for eventual certification.

Sam joined the Christopher Dock Social Studies faculty in a kind of last minute hiring. Since he had never anticipated a teaching career, his college program had not included education courses or student teaching. Since he was a first year teacher I was assigned to be his mentor, which meant I had a special responsibility to make his entry into the teaching profession as smooth as possible. His room was across the hall from mine and it fell his lot to teach a course in Canada which happened to be one that I had developed and for which I had taken a lot of ownership. I tried to be helpful by giving advice and even going as far as to give him much of the material I had used. He soon developed a good rapport with his students and capitalized well on his years of service in Africa. Yet his lack of knowledge and his inexperience in classroom management created a very uncomfortable situation. As I eavesdropped I heard his mispronunciations and inappropriate responses to student questions. I was aware of laughter as students recognized yet another faux pas and sensed his embarrassment over his inadequacy. When after three years he chose to move his family to Virginia to fulfill his passion as a tiller of the soil, I made some remarks recognizing his years with us. I began by affirming him for the positive impact he had on the lives of students in his capacity as advisor and baseball coach. I then went on to say, "There were times when I heard you thrashing in the water. I even heard gurgling sounds, but I did not think I should throw you the lifeline. I felt my best response in helping you to swim, was to shout encouragement from the shore."

Six years later Monty arrived upon the scene as another of my "mentees" and a similar scenario unfolded. I had interviewed him before he was hired and was impressed by his impeccable credentials, pleasant personality, and strong character. Though not without anxiety, he was enthusiastic and seemed ready for the challenge ahead. By the end of the first week he had reached such a level of despair that he seriously contemplated walking away from it all. Though most of his classes went as well as expected, his major problem stemmed from a few members of a particular senior class who seemed bent on breaking him in order to gain personal ego gratification. To his credit Monty "rode out the storm" by confronting the situation, and by winning their respect had things well in hand by the end of the quarter. I could truthfully say to Sam and Monty, "I understand what you're going through because I have been there too. My early floundering was very similar to yours and in some ways was even worse."

My first mentoring experience was an unofficial arrangement. In 1993 Julia Walker joined the staff as a Spanish teacher, and since my classroom was adjacent to hers I was asked to "take her under my wing." As a native of Mexico she brought a mastery of the language and a first hand knowledge of Spanish culture that served her well. Her friendliness and authenticity made her popular with students. Since her previous experience had been limited to a less structured style of tutoring, she found adjusting to classroom instruction to be extremely challenging.

In the beginning my support consisted of helping with routine details such as pronunciation of student names, taking the attendance roll, regulating room temperature, and computing and recording grades. As I got more involved on a serious level I recognized the importance of listening and providing words of encouragement. Julia was prone to frustration since she took student mischief and indifference very personally. Several times she burst into my room pleading with me to come over and get things under control. At times I found the best solution was to say, "Julia let's pray about it." After we offered audible prayers from our hearts she seemed empowered to carry on. On several occasions she came bubbling with excitement when something positive had happened and we offered prayers of praise and thanksgiving.

Julia tended to take me too seriously at times and seemed to perceive me as her overseer rather than an experienced aide. At times she was too dependent on me. Though she was at CD for only one year, I treasure my brief association with her. Her enthusiasm for life and her simple, yet profound, faith were what I needed at the time.

At the biennial Mennonite Teachers' Conventions I always enjoyed conversations with Allen, a veteran teacher of Western Mennonite and Lancaster Mennonite. Those who knew us occasionally remarked how much our teaching styles are similar. This was probably more than a coincidence, since he was the first student teacher I supervised.

In October 2003 while serving as a tour guide in the Big Valley of Central Pennsylvania, I met a man who was promoting and selling natural nutritional products. In the course of conversation I learned he was a Mennonite pastor in Cumberland County, Pennsylvania and had taught middle school social studies for a while. When we finally introduced ourselves to each other, we had a good laugh. He happened to be Paul who also served as a student teacher under my administration in the 1960s.

David was enrolled at the Philadelphia College of the Bible. As a student teacher he struggled so much that I was inclined to conclude he had chosen the wrong profession. My misgivings about possible major theological differences were misplaced and I was favorably impressed with his willingness and ability to inoffensively articulate his faith story in the context of his teaching. It was in working with him that I realized the importance of developing a good evaluation rubric to facilitate effective communication.

In looking back on my student teacher supervision my feeling are mixed. In my estimation, the link with the sponsoring colleges was weak. They did not provide much assistance in terms of expectations or feedback as things progressed. Though I gained extra time with fewer lessons to prepare and papers to grade, it required many minutes of intense conferences and assisting with various tasks. I always had a major concern that students were being used as guinea pigs and would be short changed in terms of quality education. Though my students did not make as much progress as far as mastering content, this was more than counterbalanced by the benefit of innovations and new ideas.

The satisfaction of knowing, that despite my shortcomings, I helped to equip and inspire others in their striving for excellence in the teaching profession, is a rich reward indeed.

12. CURRICULAR RELEVANCY

From the early 1960s until my 2003 retirement I filled the position of Social Studies Department chairman. In this capacity my contributions to curriculum review and revision brought me much satisfaction.

In an attempt to keep abreast of current trends in the social studies field I subscribed to professional publications, enrolled in graduate education courses, attended special seminars and workshops, visited other schools, and engaged in dialogue with other Mennonite teachers at teachers' conventions. In addition to being current, I was also concerned about providing educational experiences that fostered our Anabaptist values. As a member of the school's Curriculum Committee I was also involved in shaping the larger academic program.

For the first decade, social studies offerings were the traditional ninth grade Pennsylvania History and Civics, tenth grade World History, eleventh grade American History, and twelfth grade Problems of Democracy. In the mid-nineteen sixties things began to change. In 1963 the emphasis on Pennsylvania history was diminished and a survey of the world map as well as a unit on study skills made up the ninth grade Introductory Social Studies. In the following year POD was dropped and replaced with a semester of Economics and a semester of Government. (This was part of a national trend since a title using the word "Problems" was deemed too negative to be educationally sound.) By 1965 an elective opportunity was possible in the senior year when students chose two from the offering of Government, Economics, and Sociology.

In 1969 a significant change occurred, when with the strong encouragement of social studies major, but now supervising principal, Lee Yoder, a new approach was taken to the teaching of social studies. The 1970 yearbook gave the effort a "thumbs-up" review stating, "Revamping underclassmen history courses and introducing new teaching methods stimulated greater classroom participation. . . . Adopting new textbooks emphasized the inquiry approach and the personal investigation of subject matter by the student." In the final analysis, much was gained by recognizing the importance of the problem-solving technique in learning. However the effort met with limited success because it attempted to promote a theory without the necessary resources to make it work.

In 1973 came the big explosion as our school moved into the contemporary trend of mini-course electives. In the preceding year Bible and Social Studies departments had taken initiative, but by the 1973 school year nearly all departments were on board. Almost overnight, CD students were dazzled by the bountiful smorgasbord laid before them. In the 1973 yearbook nine different courses were listed under Roland Yoder's faculty photo. Under my name were listed Western Europe, Greece and Rome, Renaissance, Local History, American Industry, Social Trends in America, Social Reform in America, The Art of Clear Thinking, U.S. in Today's World, and American Diversity. I edged Mr. Yoder by one and set a CD record for the greatest number of courses taught in a single school year. The Social Studies Department outdid itself by developing 27 quarter course electives with as many as 22 being offered at the same time. The variety in other departments was almost equally astounding.

The following school year as a member of the Curriculum Committee I presented a review of the new format in which I listed both negative and positive factors. In the negative category

I listed problems of too much stopping and starting, more clerical work being required, more classroom materials being needed, the difficulty in scheduling classes, the possibility of overspecialization, fragmentation of course contents, and drones tending to put in time after requirements were met. I identified positive features as providing a fresh beginning with each quarter, providing a greater variety, electives giving students opportunity to choose, students getting exposure to different teachers, contents being more focused, students sensing a greater urgency to succeed and failure being less catastrophic. I concluded by saying, "At this stage the light appears to be green. No flagrant shortcomings have emerged that would give reason to curtail the present quarter electives."

During the late 1970s and throughout the 1980s things continued with little change. One significant development occurred when the Social Studies Department relinquished Family Living and Consumer Economics to the Home Economics Department that eventually changed its name to Family and Consumer Sciences.

By 1990 the faint strains of the theme "Back to Basics" was being heard. Responses to an alumni questionnaire, while still rating the Social Studies Department highly, reflected a concern about the lack of emphasis on history. In addition, several colleges failed to recognize several social studies courses with their obscure titles leaving applicants with a deficiency of credits. Though still sold on the thematic elective scheme, we added history courses in Colonial America, Civil War and Reconstruction, and Contemporary Europe.

By the late 1990s we yielded more completely to the "Back to Basics" movement and the absence of mini-course textbooks and came almost full circle. All electives were eliminated except for a selection in the senior year. Three nine-week quarters of World Cultures were required in grade nine and in grades ten and eleven students were required to take three semesters of U.S. History and a nine-week quarter of Social Issues.

I continued my efforts to promote relevancy until the very end. In my last year I offered a proposal that would require all seniors to take a semester course called Global Issues as a culmination to "fine-tune the student's preparation for post-CD challenges." It was presented as a seminar depending heavily on primary sources and Internet media resources, that would examine issues such as "use of natural resources, disparity of wealth, war and peace, trade and economic relations, injustice and abuse of power, health and welfare, population control, cultural imperialism, community versus individualism, media and propaganda, comparative religions etc."

The capstone of the CD experience is a plan known as "Building Community." It is a cooperative venture involving the Bible, English, and Social Studies departments as well as appointed personnel to oversee the senior-year events.

As chair of the Social Studies Department and co-chair of an ad hoc study committee I was engaged in helping to shape the program. In the fall of 1993 the Social Studies Department recommended the adoption of a new semester course called Social Problems. A key component was a five-day off-campus internship of community service under appropriate adult supervision. The proposal called for student initiative in making necessary contacts as well as keeping a journal and making a final oral report. In shaping the course, social studies teacher David Brubaker drew from his familiarity with a similar plan at Germantown Friends Academy where his son was enrolled. I also had conversations with persons at the Montgomery County Intermediate Unit in Norristown and had correspondence with Dr. W. C. Kashatus, director of community services at the William Penn Charter School in Philadelphia.

I submitted our proposal to the school's Curriculum Committee in October 1993, and though the concept met with general approval, action was postponed. However, in the following month a "Senior Experience" task force was appointed. Rose Lambright joined me as co-chair and social studies teachers

David Brubaker and Kirby King, Bible and science teacher Nelson Martin, student Stephen Moyer, alumna Marta Frederick Petersheim and local church leader Luke Beidler also agreed to serve. We were asked to "describe the nature, purpose, content, and evaluation of the course and detail the logistics for carrying it out."

By the end of our first meeting in December, the committee had already expanded the original proposal by giving consideration to a mini-term that would involve the entire school. Much of the impetus for this direction came from Nelson Martin who had already introduced an off-campus element in his Faith Walk class as well as an annual service day involving the total school population. He also had contact with an organization in Washington, D.C. that provided leadership for small groups seeking urban service opportunities. In addition we critiqued the mini-term program that had met with success in Western Mennonite School in Oregon.

In March 1994 Daniel Hertzler was on campus and participated in our committee discussion. He felt the primary focus should be on a project late in the senior year to capitalize on their level of maturity. This led me to introduce "The Senior Experience: A Bold New Plan" which called for an alternative educational plan for the last quarter of the senior year. It recommended granting five quarter-credits to be awarded as follows:

English	1/4 unit	(Required reading, journaling, research paper etc.)
Social Studies	1/4 unit	(Required reading, cross-cultural experiences, lectures and research on social problems etc.)
Bible	1/4 unit	(Required reading, journaling about personal spiritual pilgrimage, and projects encouraging servanthood etc.)
Science	1/4 unit	(Required reading, enviro-ethics, visit greenhouses, zoos, farms etc.)

Creative Arts   1/4 unit   (Producing a drama or music program; attend concerts; visit museums, apprenticeship in painting, sculpture, and architecture; projects related to clothing, food, home furnishings and renovations etc.)

In the end this scheme was seen as unrealistic because of issues pertaining to athletics and impact on yearlong courses like calculus and physics.

In May 1994 the Senior Experience Committee made a presentation that included elements of the "Nelson Martin Omnibus" plan and the original Social Studies Department recommendation. The introduction of the report stated:

> After due consideration the committee was unanimous in affirming the concept of incorporating a non-traditional dimension relating to service and community building into our curriculum. Though going beyond the original call, the committee was also unanimous in the strong belief that instead of merely devising a component to be added during the senior year, it was imperative to build something into each of the four grades, with the most significant event occurring during the senior year. For grade nine the proposal calls for two days and a night in an informal camp early in the year with activities under the direction of the Guidance Department. Grade ten calls for a 12-hour service requirement in the context of the sophomore Bible class. For grade eleven students shall be given two weeks of released time from scheduled classes for varied off-campus service (or job shadowing) options. In grade 12, students would take the quarter course on Social Problems and devote the last five school days for a culminating group experience.

On November 23, 1994 Meg Mann, director of the Washington, D.C. Presbyterian Seminar Center, attended a special session of the Curriculum Committee and other interested persons. She introduced the program, gave a slide presentation and responded to questions of concern.

With the exception of flipping the recommendations for grades eleven and twelve, the Curriculum Committee endorsed the task force's proposal and asked the committee to stay with the project and develop a more concrete plan for the senior year. After some fine-tuning the final product followed a three-phase scheme that included a five-day service or job shadowing project, and an off-campus outing at a winter camp in mid-January as well as a culminating public presentation in June by each graduate. (For a more complete study of CD's "Building Community" program see the excellent review by J. Eric Bishop and Sharon Fransen in the September 1998 issue of *Phi Delta Kappan*.)

Today CD's "Building Community" has become an integral part of the total school program and is held in high esteem by participants and observers alike.

13. SABBATICALS

In 1967 at the urging of Principal Yoder, the Board of Trustees initiated a sabbatical leave plan for CD teachers and administrators. Though many educational institutions have abandoned their sabbatical provisions, sensing its importance for morale and enrichment, the CD Board has wisely retained this benefit. During the last several decades, a pattern has emerged in which two members of the faculty and administration take advantage of the opportunity each year. During my tenure at CD I was granted four sabbatical leaves. (They should really be called "decadicals" instead of sabbaticals since they were bestowed every ten years instead of seven.) These experiences not only provided necessary changes of pace, but stimulated tremendous personal growth that contributed significantly to my teaching success.

As a charter member of the CD faculty, Daniel Reinford qualified as the first sabbatical candidate. However, his plans were such that he preferred to wait until 1969–1970 and he graciously deferred to me. The opportunity took me by surprise, but after much pondering, I decided to take the bold step. I submitted a proposal that met with quick approval. It called for spending the 1968–1969 school year in travel and study in Europe.

My first matter of business was to find a university where I could enroll for the academic year. Because of the language factor, a British school seemed the best choice. Using materials found in the library at Temple University, I identified possibilities. I applied to eleven British universities and received a favorable response from eight. Lured by the enchantment of Scotland, I enrolled in a non-degree program at the university in the charming seacoast town of St. Andrews.

July 24 found Naomi and me aboard the S.S. Statendam bound for Rotterdam. From there we began our two-month "grand tour" of Europe. Along the way we collected many post cards, brochures, and souvenirs and took many pictures for classroom use. Of much greater significance, was the life changing input of the charming cities, spectacular scenery, and friendly people in the seventeen countries we visited.

On October 4 I registered for classes in the ancient University of St. Andrews. Since one of my goals was to study the American Revolution from the British perspective, I enrolled in courses in Modern British History and Modern European History. In order to better understand the culture of the region, I also took a course in Scottish History. I found the British education system to be quite different. Though not true in my case, I observed the pressure students felt as they were "sitting exams" that exclusively determined their academic future. All class sessions involved lectures without any student participation. However, each class had weekly tutorials where students met in small groups to discuss course content and "defend" their written work.

One of the most significant parts of my education abroad was a three-week excursion with 23 British students behind the "Iron Curtain" in Poland and Russia. When I blended in with the other students in the group things went smoothly. On one occasion I cast inhibitions aside, and with other male "Brits", danced the Watusi with some Russian girls. However, when they saw my German name or heard my American accent I felt some tension as I was given closer scrutiny. A number of times I was asked the haunting question: "Why don't you Americans like us?"

As in other countries visited, I observed both good and bad. A physical and psychological pall seemed to persist and the ever-present watchdog bands of soldiers gave evidence of limited personal freedom. Yet, the impeccable chandelier-lit subways, splendor of the Hermitage in Leningrad, and the moving performance of *Sleeping Beauty* in Moscow's Bolshoi Theatre profoundly impressed me.

On a gray April morning I found myself part of a queue, three blocks long, walking four-deep to get a quick glimpse of the embalmed corpse of Vladimir Lenin as he lay in a glass enclosure. That occasion was an Easter that takes on an increasingly deeper meaning as I contrast the joy of serving a risen Christ to the tragic adulation of a dead and now discredited hero.

Since I was not working toward a degree at St. Andrews, my academic program was less rigorous and less structured. We put many miles on our new Ford Cortina as we "soaked up" the culture and the land of Scotland. Though I did not invest in a bagpipe or a kilt with all its accoutrements, I did come back with an impressive collection of slides and a repertoire of Scottish ballads. Most important, however, were the memories and the friendships we formed that are still warmly maintained today.

My second sabbatical was quite different from the first. Over a number of years I had developed a growing interest in genealogy and had collected volumes of data. I received considerable encouragement to engage in further research, compile my information, and present it in printed form. This appealed to me so I applied to the Board Of Trustees for a 1978–1979 sabbatical with this as my primary goal. Since this request was unique, action on my request was delayed. Finally an agreement was reached in which I would also take some additional graduate courses.

During the year, I traveled to Ohio, Missouri, Nebraska, and Oregon, making contact with "long-lost" relatives. I made several trips to the National Archives in Washington, D.C. and visited scores of courthouses and historical libraries. I engaged in extensive correspondence in obtaining family information and photos. In the fall of 1980 Gateway Press published a 282-page book with 192 photographs, entitled *Christian Kauffman: His Descendants and His People.*

For my other phase I enrolled in the College of Education at Temple University. I took a valuable course in Recent Trends in Social Studies Education that affirmed our school's mini-course electives approach. For my major project I developed a quarter course in Thanatology (study of death) to be added to the CD curriculum. My other two courses were part of a program providing certification for department chairs and curriculum supervisors. Though I "aced" the courses, I did not find them all that helpful, and never followed through in completing the remaining program requirements.

My third sabbatical consisted of another major writing project. The Mifflin County Mennonite Historical Society was looking for someone to write a history of the local Amish and Mennonites as part of a bicentennial celebration of the first arrivals. Though it was ambitious, I had interest, so I applied for a 1988–1989 sabbatical with that in mind. Principal Peachey had Mifflin County roots and that likely helped in receiving approval.

Travel again was a key component. I went to Ohio, Indiana, Illinois, Kansas, Nebraska, and Ontario as I traced Amish migrations from Mifflin County. I spent many hours in local historical libraries and courthouses. I devoted three weeks to scanning old newspapers on microfilm in the state library in Harrisburg searching for local human-interest stories.

In addition to the research and writing, I visited local congregations promoting the project and doing some fund-raising to subsidize printing costs. The fruit of my labor resulted in a 472-page book entitled *The Mifflin County Amish and Mennonite Story*. Its quality exceeded my highest expectations and the demand was such that within nine years another printing was necessary. This effort not only sharpened my research and writing skills, but also gave me a better understanding and appreciation of the Anabaptist heritage.

As another decade drew to a close I debated whether I should ask for a sabbatical leave for 1998–1999. I already had three and my service would likely not go beyond another three or four years. I decided to proceed with another request, but at the same time I was resigned to the possibility of its being rejected. I submitted a modified plan that asked for a leave for one semester instead of the entire year. In my application I said, "I believe the change of pace and opportunities for professional enrichment will benefit me personally and make my last years more productive. I am also convinced that the school's educational program will be enhanced by the activities I would like to do during my semester's leave." My proposed activities included travel in Europe, improving my computer skills, and curriculum review and evaluation.

In April and May, Naomi and I spent a delightful four weeks in Southwest England, Wales and Scotland. Technologically I made a big step by putting my "Apple IIE aside and replacing it with a Dell PC with Windows 98.

My most significant activity, however, was time spent reviewing our present social studies curriculum and in an attempt to work at eventual coordination, visiting Quakertown Christian and Penn View Christian to get a better feel for what was happening there. In reviewing their curricula and consulting with their social studies personnel, I discovered some significant gaps and duplications that gave us direction in making revisions for our 2000–2001 school year. The contacts were also beneficial in laying the foundation for a greater degree of cooperation among the three schools.

14. CHAPELS

One unique feature that reflects the school's priorities and sets it apart from most is its regular schedule of chapels. According to my calculation I was involved in approximately 4,300 chapels at Christopher Dock. On most occasions I sat in the audience. However, in other incidences I spent time up front engaged in a more direct form of participation.

There were times when I was involved in special music performances. I have fond memories of the various faculty quartets of which I was a part. Occasionally we presented several songs in the chapel setting. I particularly enjoyed it, when around Christmas; Eleanor Ruth would join us in *The Star and the Wise Men*. Once in a while I sang the Christmas ballad *The Friendly Beasts*. During the 1970s and 1980s my fellow Mifflin County transplant, math teacher Jerry Yoder and I would bring our guitars and spend entire chapel periods singing sets of Gospel songs.

Along the way I gave approximately 30 chapel talks. Many are long forgotten and justifiably so. However, in going through my files, I found a dozen that I must have felt were worth saving. In reading them I discovered that today I would question some of my earlier conclusions.

On three occasions I was asked to give the first chapel talk for the new school year. In the case of one entitled *My Vision for the New Year*, I began by doing a take-off on Martin Luther King, Junior's *I Have a Dream*. I got the students' attention and a great deal of laughter, but I regret what I did because the levity was in extremely poor taste. Some topics were quite far out such as *Sleeping Preachers and the Charismatic Movement* and *Triskaidekaphobia and His Cousins* delivered on Friday October 13. I spent considerable time on one entitled *Boo-Boos* in which I ended with the question, "Why not give a bungler a break?" In the spring of 1968 I gave my $60 chapel talk, *The Rebel's Code,* which ended up in *With* magazine and later in two other religious publications. (See *Appendix.*) I devoted the most time and energy to *An Analysis of Adolescent Reading Trends* in which I polled 125 CD students and visited neighborhood newsstands, bookstores, and libraries. My last chapel presentation called for the most courage, when in my Colonial outfit, without notes, I presented a monologue about the man Christopher Dock, portrayed through Christopher Sauer, one of his students.

By some strange twist I developed a reputation for the style and content of my prayers in chapel. On one occasion I was flabbergasted when my concluding "Amen" was followed by applause. It felt good, but I was uncomfortable with the possibility I had crossed the line of impropriety.

Prayer is conversation with God. I firmly believe in the power of prayer and have witnessed answered prayers. However, I have always had some problems with leading out in a public prayer. Do I present my personal agenda while the audience merely listens in? Do I try to determine the consensus of the group and pray accordingly? What if I'm not at the same place? What do I do if there are differences within the group? I might thank God for the refreshing rain that pleased the gardeners, while there are some in the audience that are angry because their barbeque was rained out. I have come to the place where I attempt to address God personally on behalf of those assembled, but with the understanding that those who cannot say "Amen" to my requests or objects of praise, should tune me out and offer their silent personal amendments. I have also decided to use my own style, and since the Creator of the Platypus obviously has a sense of humor, He won't mind if I spice up my prayers a bit from time to time.

During the last eight years it has become a tradition to open each chapel with an invocation in which four or five students are identified, and prayer is offered on their behalf. This was a commendable practice. However, in many cases the prayers were generic expressions with names merely tacked on. On one occasion, a student was named along with the other four, and the words that followed were extremely inappropriate because that particular student had transferred to another school a month before.

Since I was informed of the names in advance, I made it a point to be very specific in the prayers I offered. In order to pray intelligently, without divulging my motive, I tried to engage the students in conversation during the days before the event. I also checked out the "Student Profile" in the Guidance Office to gain information about their special interests and activities in which they were involved. On the occasion I tried to present something affirming and worthy of praise as well as offer petitions on their behalf.

As I reflect on chapel experiences from the pew my feelings are somewhat mixed. There were times when I had problems accepting some things—especially the "music" of some of the talent chapels of the 1990s that, by my standard, did not seem conducive to worship. Though tempted to walk out in protest, I restrained myself. It was helpful for me to remind myself that the music of my youth shocked the older generation as much as this performance was upsetting me.

My final grade for CD chapels would be very high. We were fortunate to be challenged by guest preachers, missionaries, and educators. Spiritual Life Emphasis Weeks, with few exceptions, brought the campus community together in times of renewal. Chapels with the greatest impact were often those by alumni who returned sharing their personal pilgrimages.

The thing that impressed me the most was the extent and quality of student participation. Students volunteered to serve on chapel planning committees. Many assumed responsibility for leading devotions or singing. The most unforgettable chapels occurred when students made themselves vulnerable as they shared their struggles and resolved to take a new direction in life. In February 1990, when I was somewhat disillusioned after returning from a sabbatical, I distributed a paper to the faculty in which I addressed the issue of chapel programming. Among my recommendations were more faculty participation; drafting a statement of philosophy and set of objectives; creating a special chapel committee consisting of students, faculty, parents, and alumni; and giving more attention to long range planning which would place more emphasis on themes that would provide greater continuity. In time all of these would be adopted, but my last suggestion, which promoted the idea of making attendance at one all-student chapel each week voluntary, failed to muster sufficient support.

15. IS MY FACE RED?

On two different occasions school yearbook captions commented on how I disliked being embarrassed. Apparently students were aware of times when this occurred. At this point I do not recall many, suggesting they must have been of a minor nature or I have succeeded in submerging them in the deep recesses of my memory. However, there are a lingering few that still make me squirm when I recall them.

A recurring source of embarrassment throughout my teaching days was my inability to tell one twin from the other. I had no problem with Mark and Marlin, Jay and Ray, Bruce and Brian, Jen and Janelle, or Rick and Rodney, but distinguishing Mary from Martha, Jim from John, Sarah from Megan, Geoff from Jason, Jeremy from Jared, or Amanda from Abigail was something I never mastered.

Of course there were incidents pertaining to appearance such as the occasional open fly, the mismatched pair of brown and black shoes or the indiscreet six-inch rip in the seat of my trousers. There were mistakes in checking papers. Sometimes right answers were marked wrong and vice-versa due to lack of adequate concentration. At times the key was wrong which had a catastrophic ripple effect. Then there were the misspellings and "typos." These were usually a result of haste and carelessness but in some cases to my shame, I eventually found I had been misspelling certain words for years. I spelled temperance, "temperence;" judgment, "judgement;" siege, "seige;" and Niagara,

"Niagra," and there may have been others that my present spell-check would reveal.

A typing blunder that caused considerable embarrassment occurred in my course in Ancient Greece and Rome. While students were taking a test, Steve raised his hand and asked, "Did you really mean to say what you did in the third discussion question?" I then read the question and assured him that I did. At that point he walked up to the desk and pointed out my blooper and I almost fainted. I had given a discussion question in which I had asked the students to describe the city of Athens and to be sure to "describe in detail the public area." Unfortunately I had forgotten to include the letter "l" in the word public. When the matter was disclosed there were some in the class that howled in laughter, but I was also surprised by the number who "never got it" suggesting a possible void in their sex education.

One day after class, Tina came up to me in a very agitated condition. She said, "Why don't you like me?" I replied, "Why do you ask a question like that?" She responded, "I copied everything on this paper word for word from Lois. You gave her a B and me a C." She obviously had me "over the barrel." All I could say was, "It looks like both of us have something we have to work at."

One of my stupidest goofs occurred during my first summer while I was working with Elton Meyers in campus maintenance. The school had a large walk-behind, self-propelled mower with several extra gangs attached. The challenge of maneuvering the contraption was such that Meyers was reluctant to trust me with it. What happened during the first hour of my effort justified his concern. On the breast of the dam of the school pond there was a hole deep and wide as a result of the planned installation of a new overflow pipe. Though he warned me explicitly to avoid it, I managed to soon have the entire rig resting deep within its bowels. He uttered very few words, but I will long remember his sweat and grunts as we labored several hours getting it out.

In my first week at CD I was umpiring a boy's softball game when Carl, the pitcher, stopped abruptly in the middle of his wind-up evoking cries of "balk" from the opposing team. Though I had officiated softball before, I was unable to sort this one out. Finally I indeed did call it a balk, allowing all runners to advance, and for good measure even sent the batter to first base. Though I was embarrassed by my indecision of the moment, I was humiliated even more when Carl brought in his rulebook the following day that showed that in softball a balk infraction didn't even exist.

One day not long ago I took my place to supervise students in the library. As I settled things down at the beginning of the period I noticed some students who were not on the seating chart. Assuming they were there from another class for checking out books, I asked them why they did not have the required pass. To taunting laughter I was informed that I was in the wrong study hall. This mistake was somewhat understandable. It had occurred shortly after periods eight and nine had been switched to lessen the impact of early dismissal for students engaged in athletic events.

Another incident, which caused considerable shame and remorse, happened when I had endured enough of the boisterous conduct in the room across the hall. I was especially upset because the teacher frequently left his classroom unsupervised and the students would soon be in an uproar. On this occasion I stormed into the room and really gave them a "royal chewing out" only to discover after my tirade that the teacher was standing in the far corner of the room. I simply walked out, saving my apology for later.

One afternoon as I was teaching students about the Maritime Provinces of Canada it seemed to be one of my better days. Students were paying close attention and were volunteering answers to my questions. I even engaged them in some higher level thinking by capitalizing on the harsh climate of Newfoundland as an opportunity to discuss the relationship of geography to culture. After half the period had gone, a student raised his hand and said, "Mr. Kauffman this is your China class, not Canada!" At that point I was so incapacitated I had to sit down in order to compose myself. I was so unnerved that I did not even try to go to China that period. What happened? I had spent the lunch period brushing up on my Canada presentation and when the bell rang I was psyched for that and moved right into the discussion in period seven when I should have saved it for period eight.

An incident more strange than embarrassing occurred in G-3. While standing in the front of the classroom I felt a strange movement on my shoulder. Assuming someone was tapping to get my attention I turned, but to my surprise nobody was there. The movement persisted. Before I could check out my suspicion, the mouse under my coat ran down my leg and scurried out the door, evoking shrieks of horror from the surprised observers. Later I discovered the mouse had been under duress since it was being chased by the maintenance man in the hallway and chose my corpus as a sanctuary. Though it left me in a shaken condition, I was grateful that it had chosen the outside rather than the inside of my trouser leg in its retreat.

16. SOME PET PEEVES

My long tenure at Christopher Dock High School reflected a general state of personal contentment. However there were occasional circumstances involving both students and teachers that aggravated me. Admittedly they were vexations rather than episodes or trends that caused debilitating distress. Though recognizing the probability that I also caused grief for others, and conceding that some are of the nit-picking variety, I am offering two lists of my top ten pet peeves.

STUDENTS WHO:

1. **Exhibited drowsiness**
    As disclosed earlier, I took it personally when students displayed signs that sleep was about to overtake them. I demonstrated leniency in extenuating circumstances such as medication, but in other cases I took bold action sometimes described as drastic.

2. **Missed assignment deadlines**
    I tried very hard to give explicit instructions with my assignments. I provided sufficient time to accomplish the task and gave constant verbal and written reminders of the dates the materials were due. I considered flaunting deadlines to be a reflection of a serious character deficiency.

3. Were absent on test days

I conducted several different statistical analyses that proved absenteeism was forty to fifty per cent higher on the day of a test compared to an ordinary day. For some students, absence on testing days was predictable. I felt taken advantage of because of the extra burden it placed on me. It meant extra time in administering the late test and in cases where dishonesty was suspected, creating a different version. Doubly perturbing was the tendency of some to drag things out by failing to take initiative to make up a missed test or assignment.

4. Copied other student's work

Despite clear expectations, assignments were submitted that gave evidence they were not original with the student. In some cases I was not without fault, since my worksheets in particular, made it easy to yield to temptation to copy. If I discovered matching papers I usually gave both parties a zero. There were times when I gave half-credit if one student had done all the original work. Though plagiarism was always a challenge in research paper evaluation, computer Internet resources have made it even more difficult. Without a doubt some slipped past me, but on several occasions the literary style was so blatantly unique that detection was simple. On one occasion a social studies colleague and I refused to accept a doctored document that led to a student's failure to receive his diploma.

5. Refused to carry their weight in group activities

As a traditionalist I did not provide many opportunities for cooperative learning. I had a problem coping with the inequities that resulted from the drones that expected the others to be worker bees. Yet, the indolent and irresponsible expected the same grade and were quick to gloat about the final product.

6. Failed to bring their textbooks to class

Certain students developed a pattern of coming to perform a

task without bringing the proper tools. Some openly flaunted the reading assignment by leaving their textbook in the rack under the desk or on a table nearby. I never developed a consistent way of dealing with the problem. Since I disliked losing the five or six minutes it took when I sent them to their locker, I usually took a pragmatic approach by having extra copies available for their use. I did note some improvement when I took it into consideration in evaluating class participation.

7. Wasted time during "open study"

I never was completely sold on the concept of permitting students with good grades to go outdoors or to another unsupervised designated place during their study period. I had some concern about the philosophical justification, but my major complaint was the abuse of the policy by students who slept, sunned, and socialized instead of engaging in an academic activity.

8. Emitted audible yawns

As a teacher I did not see a yawn in a positive light since I tended to associate it with boredom. At times it was a result of a lack of oxygen that cast a reflection on temperature and ventilation factors in the room. I recognized that yawns were involuntary responses beyond control and tried to ignore them. However, when the yawn was accompanied by a sound from the vocal cords, it was a disruption I did not disregard.

9. Refused to sing in chapel

Allowing for the fact that some could not sing well, it was my observation that many students in school choirs for some reason didn't share their talents in the larger group setting. They were consistently silent regardless of the type of song that was being sung. I am glad to say this annoyance had gradually diminished as student attitudes and chapel participation improved.

10. Sniffled while taking a test

When students were quietly taking a test I was often bothered when the silence was broken by a student's uncivilized, unconscious pattern of sniffling sinus drippings and congested matter. It often seemed extremely incongruous since those engaging in the practice considered themselves to be models of sophistication. A supply of free tissues was always at their disposal.

TEACHERS WHO:

1. Passed on their discipline cases to me as detention supervisor.

Detention hall was originally intended for students who were tardy or needed some time-out because of a lunchtime infraction. As it turned out, more students were there for classroom misconduct than any other reason. In some cases new teachers that did not understand the system sent them, or on other occasions, by those who panicked at a critical moment. Sometimes it seemed like persons "passed the buck" instead of assuming responsibility for their sphere of jurisdiction.

2. Were lax in their supervision obligation.

On-campus supervising was one of the least glamorous teacher responsibilities. Though the general level of commitment was commendable, there were occasions, when due to forgetfulness or indifference, some assignments were not filled.

3. Allowed students to go to the Media Center to put in time.

Libraries are intended to be quiet places for reading and research. While supervising there, I dealt with too many students with signed passes that had no interest in serious study. They took up limited space and often caused disturbance.

4. Were late to class.

For a host of reasons some teachers often failed to make it to their classroom on time. Sometimes it was a result of the long distance. It might have been a conversation with a student. Perhaps it was the pain of tearing away from the stimulating banter of the faculty lounge or the necessary last-minute printing job. This tardiness did not set a good tone for classroom management and sometimes neighboring teachers suffered because of the hoard of students milling around the locked door.

5. Got off the subject or bogged down discussion.

At times faculty meetings or committee sessions were prolonged because discussion meandered or included irrelevant comments. I was inclined to view such meetings as a time for business rather than a social occasion. When I was called to be a facilitator I tried hard to keep matters on track. My fanaticism in this regard even led me to make a bold move to halt a rambling discourse in a faculty meeting even when I was not in charge. I simply broke in, raised my forefinger, and boldly declared, "One more minute!" In this isolated case, my semi-rude, unconventional interception worked.

6. Were late to faculty and committee meetings.

Latecomers inevitably caused a disruption when they arrived. They often missed early items of business and in some cases expected a recapitulation in order to be brought up to date. This, as well as a delayed start on their behalf, sometimes caused a later dismissal for everybody.

7. Cluttered up the teacher's workroom.

It would be an over-statement to say I avoided the faculty workroom because it was so depressing. Yet I will say that a floor covered with paper punch-outs and counters with sheets of paper strewn about created an aura that did not give my spirits a boost.

8. Allowed students to continue taking a test after the bell had rung.

Some students work at a slower pace and as a result more

time may be required for taking a test. However, allowing the students to stay for several minutes to complete the work had an impact on the next class. In my case, if they arrived five minutes late they missed my announcements or "bell-ringer" question. Sometimes the discussion had already started and it was hard for them to get on board. My biggest frustration occurred when I began the period with a pop quiz and the student arrived after most of the class had already finished.

9. Caused a copy machine breakdown and then fled

The school has done well in providing technology for print duplication. However there were too many times when I patiently waited through "warm-up" only to find the copier to be inoperable. Sometimes it was a paper jam. On other occasions the supply of powder or liquid was depleted. If the person using the device when it broke down would have posted a little sign or reported it to the office staff, considerable grief would have been avoided.

10. Gave tests and set deadlines on the same date as mine

It often seemed to happen that when I gave a test, other teachers followed suit. When I had them working on a research paper or reading a paperback, other teachers were doing the same. Though the old system of signing up at a central place to space out major tests proved impractical, some plan to inform each other of our test and major assignment schedule would have been helpful.

17. TEAM CAPTAINS

A major factor in the remarkable success of Christopher Dock Mennonite High School was the outstanding leadership of its administrators. Each brought managerial gifts that seemed right for their particular period in the school's history.

Nobody deserves more credit for the school's enviable reputation than Principal Richard C. Detweiler. In my estimation he epitomized the qualities of Colonial schoolmaster Christopher Dock better than anyone I have ever known. Though confronted with many complex challenges, his unflappable demeanor was a constant source of reassurance that all would be well. In maintaining discipline he did not show anger or resort to harsh punishment. He was so loved and respected that the recognition of his disappointment, in itself, brought shame and a resolution to reform. Dave, who on one occasion was sent to the Principal's office for misbehavior, tells the story. As it happened, Mr. Detweiler engaged Dave in casual conversation about the family store and the state of the Phillies and dismissed him without ever mentioning his reason for coming.

When you were with him, his capacity to care was so authentic that at the moment, you felt like you were the only interest he had. I personally owe him a great debt of gratitude. I am indebted to him for bringing me to CD as well as retaining me after my two-year commitment was complete. During my first week he took me into his family at Perkasie until my final boarding plans were complete. He stood by me when my perceived

liberalism was under attack. After my second year, I actually submitted my resignation hoping to get into a public school in
Chester County where my wife was already employed. He even
allowed me to use his office phone to set up interviews. He kept
my position open for me at CD and hired me back when my job
search failed and even helped my wife to find employment in the
Pennridge School District.

Lee Yoder, a fellow product of Mifflin County, started out
as my colleague in the Social Studies Department, but he was
soon tapped and groomed for bigger things. In replacing
Detweiler as CD's chief administrator, it was soon apparent that
his style was quite different. Lee had been a certified basketball
referee in earlier days and he brought that no-nonsense, technical-
foul-calling approach to his new position. Despite his Amish
roots, he displayed a remarkable capacity for open-mindedness
and flexibility as he steered the course through the turbulent
1960s and '70s. The chief quality of his leadership was its boldness. He dared to take risks and seize opportunities when they
emerged. Few will ever know of the vision, astuteness, and dedication he demonstrated in the million-dollar, 108-acre land
purchase, that not only provided for the school's campus expansion, but also made possible the birth of the neighboring Dock
Woods Community. On one occasion he addressed the CD
faculty with the challenge to "develop a curriculum having
contemporary characteristics in the context of a Christian philosophy of education." As a result, momentum was generated
for the adoption of a wide variety of more relevant short-term
electives.

The Paul Miller administration should be recognized for the
progress made in renovating and expanding the school's physical
facilities. This included a brand-new classroom building dubbed
Dielman Hall and extensive work on old Grebel Hall and the
structure used for an auditorium, cafeteria, and gymnasium that
would then be christened Clemens Center. In the spirit of optimism, an earlier master plan was dusted off as department chairs

were asked to dream and project their needs and expectations for a student enrollment of 500.

Paul's unflagging zeal, indefatigable effort, and communication skills contributed mightily to the success of these projects. However, his last two years were tense for both him and the faculty. Much went on behind the scenes of which I had no knowledge, but from my observation, it would seem that his focus on construction was so intense that he lost touch with the faculty. Efforts to heal the rift were unsuccessful which led to his departure after five years.

Aside from my 1958–'59 greenhorn year, the 1977–1978 school year was the most troubling for me. Serving as a faculty representative on the Administrative Council, I found myself caught in the middle. In interviews with the board and conversations with Paul, I attempted to reflect the feelings of my faculty constituency. Yet, I found myself drawn into the matter in a personal way that led to some regrettable attitudes and actions on my part.

After serving as Assistant Principal under both Yoder and Miller, in the fall of 1979, Elam Peachey began his eleven-year stint as Principal of Christopher Dock High School. I had a very comfortable relationship with him since we had been schoolmates at Belleville Mennonite School. He had also been married to my second cousin who was tragically killed in an auto accident a few days before their third wedding anniversary leaving him with a daughter who was less than two years old.

Elam's strength lay in his management skills. While placing a high priority on efficiency, he avoided becoming a control freak by devising proper connecting links and delegating responsibility to others. During his incumbency he gave staff development maximum attention, utilizing professional resource persons for in-service training. Under his encouragement the school took the technological leap into the age of computerization.

After Elam's unexpected 1990 resignation and subsequent acceptance of a position in Development at Hesston College in Kansas, the mantle of leadership fell on the shoulders of Elaine

Left to right: Gerald Benner, Elaine Moyer, Duane Kauffman with clock crafted by Abe Schmitt given to Kauffman in recognition of 35 years of service at Christopher Dock High School

Aeshliman Moyer who was serving as Acting Principal while Peachey was on sabbatical leave completing work for his doctorate. Though women in administrative roles still raised many eyebrows, she assumed command with a firm hand and soon won the admiration of the various segments of the school community. During the twelve years I served on her team I was especially impressed by her greater degree of visibility on campus, professional appearance, poise under pressure, and sensitivity to many voices.

In addition to these five, Harvey W. Bauman, Carroll Moyer, and Ronald Hertzler also served as acting or interim principal. When Harvey brought his 23 years of Lancaster County administration and teaching experience to CD he was actually given the title of "principal" as he served under Richard Detweiler the Supervising Principal. By his own admission, he was not cut out for the "nuts and bolts" of administrative duties. In his fifth year as principal he resigned and went back to his first love that was teaching. With his diverse knowledge, common sense, and deep passion for his "young people," during the next seventeen years he made an incalculable impact on the lives of many students. However, toward the end of his service, his failing health and energy, created frustration that led to self-debasement and diminished effectiveness. As an observer, it seemed to me he had "remained in the saddle" a little too long and I resolved not to let it happen to me. A month before his death I visited him in his home. As I left, he gave me a fatherly hug and with tears in his eyes said, "Duane, it is going to be up to people like you to turn things around."

It is unlikely that anyone has worn more hats at CD than Carroll Moyer. After eleven years in the public schools of Illinois, he joined the Christopher Dock faculty in 1961. Two years later he was appointed Assistant Principal. For the next seven years, in addition to teaching and guidance responsibility, he served in that capacity. In the year before Lee Yoder began his term as Supervising Principal, Carroll assumed the bulk of administrative responsibility. He was the school's first full-fledged Guidance Counselor, assuming that role in 1974, finally getting his own office and secretary when Dielman Hall was completed in 1978. In addition to 25 years of classroom teaching and 16 years as Guidance Counselor, he served capably as *Dockument* advisor, chair of two steering committees for Middle States Accrediting Association self studies, founder and advisor for the National Honor Society, audio-visual coordinator, and drama coach, as well as important roles on PTF and School Activities Committees. During his last sabbatical in 1981 he made a bold move by enrolling in Kutztown University for certification in Library Science. For the next nine years he served as Director of the Media Center at Christopher Dock. His good voice, "patented laugh," language skills, and poise served him well as moderator of many public events.

I personally valued his friendship. As baseball fans we were constantly ribbing each other since we rooted for opposing teams. I also enjoyed several years of standing beside him as we made our contributions to the bass section in the Penn Valley Men's chorus.

Spanning the years of all the CD administrators was the indispensable contribution of Eleanor Ruth. For over four decades she heroically balanced the needs of administration, faculty, and students as she combined the roles of office secretary, administrative assistant, and receptionist. Her organizational skills, composed demeanor, and relentless dedication provided inestimable stability and continuity. Though I received occasional memos chiding me for negligence in maintaining my textbook inventory or failure to collect money for lost textbooks, we worked well together and I cherish our friendship very highly.

18. TEAMMATES

When I arrived during the high school's fifth year, I was very impressed by the serious approach to academics. Much of this was the result of the tone set by charter faculty members Janet Martin and Pearl Schrack. While stretched into responsibilities outside their spheres of preparation, they demonstrated a competence and professionalism that won the admiration of students and faculty alike. Though they no doubt looked askance at my early fumbling, instead of disparagement, I received nothing but their full support.

Under Janet's capable leadership the Commercial Department soon developed a reputation for producing top-notch secretaries and accountants for local businesses. Pearl laid the foundation for an English Department that has consistently served as the flagship for the others.

Students privileged to have been in Daniel Reinford's German or math classes were almost unanimous in their praise. They received more than course content. They also acquired valuable lessons in perspective and self-discipline. His friar-like appearance belied his keen intellect and subtle humor. His dark eyes would sparkle after he had stumped me one more time with one of his riddles. As he moved about on campus he displayed a sense of urgency by choosing to trot rather than saunter at a more leisurely pace. As a teammate I can also vouch for the fact that accuracy was not only applied to his mathematical equations, but also to his two-handed set-shots from near half-court in the old gymnasium.

When Al Martin arrived straight from Goshen College to teach for his 1-W service, we seemed to click immediately. Perhaps I bonded with him because I saw my earlier self as he began his teaching career. One big thing that linked us was our baseball fanaticism. Since he rooted for the Red Sox and I was a Dodger fan, our interests did not conflict. We traveled to Philadelphia, New York City, Boston, Baltimore, and Washington, D.C. where we not only enjoyed the games, but also learned a few things about the facts of life.

In Boston a "tonic" almost got us into trouble. While we were duckpin bowling at Fenway Park Al almost got us tossed out because he failed to comply with the order to remove his drink from the seat at the alley approach. If the manager would have said soft drink, pop, or soda, there would have been no problem, but neither of us had a clue about what he meant when he called it a tonic. One occasion after a game at Yankee Stadium, we ended up spending the night at the Bronx YMCA and as a couple of country boys we learned very quickly about culture in the urban red-light district.

One night while we were at a game in old Connie Mack Stadium in Philadelphia, I learned the truth of Dostoevsky's assertion that "the criminal mind lurks inside each of us," when in the exuberance of celebrating a Koufax no-hitter I assaulted a boy in the row in front of me with a rolled up sheet of paper and proceeded, in one of the most regrettable moments of my life, to mishandle badly a confrontation with his father.

From 1954 to 1957 Roland Yoder and I were both belonged to the Zelathian Literary Society at Eastern Mennonite College, but since we did not have any classes together, or sing in the same choir, or play on the same softball team we did not really get to know each other that well. After he joined the CD faculty in 1960 that changed, and in time our relationship was so strong that when Dottie and he went to Ethiopia for a year, they entrusted Naomi and me with maintaining their house, lawn and garden. After 39 years together on the CD faculty I had the privilege of

Singing *"The Big Little Man of CD"* at Roland Yoder's 1999 retirement reception, Jerold Yoder on left

presenting a tribute in the form of a ballad, *Big Little Man of CD,* which I sang on the occasions of his April retirement recognition and June 1999 retirement reception. (See *Appendix 5.*)

The quality of a school can usually be judged by the degree of support it receives from its alumni. In this respect, Christopher Dock High School stands tall. 58 of its former students have returned for a time of service on its staff. The first was Naomi Kolb (DuBlanica) of the class of 1958 who joined the CD faculty as a math teacher in 1961. The following year Eileen Moyer (Viau) came as a Spanish, German, and phys-ed instructor. Since that time eighteen other CD graduates have returned to their alma mater as classroom teachers.

In 1965 Gerald Benner from the class of 1959 accepted responsibility for teaching upper level English. He not only maintained the high Schrack and Martin standards, but under his leadership the English Department developed a reputation for excellence in the realm of oral expression. Teaching across the hall, I was often envious of the hoopla generated by his students' "demonstration speeches." You might want to ask him about the time one of these speeches brought a concerned policeman to the campus.

In the fall of 1990 or 1991, while walking together on the moors near Laurelville, Gerald confided that he was pondering the possibility of making a significant career change. He said he was feeling stale and in a rut and was considering taking advantage of another CD assignment that might come his way. I do not recall my reaction. To me he was a veteran teacher of twenty-five years with things well in hand and I honestly was not sure he was assertive enough for the new challenge. He surprised me by doing something I never did. While in the "woods" he dared to choose the other path. In the 1992–'93 school year he returned as Director of Development and in that capacity, by knowing the community and demonstrating a knack for the correct approach, he has contributed admirably to the school's continuing growth.

In the fall of 1978 the CD faculty got its "Energizer Dummy" that has just kept going, going, and going. In 1973 Eric Bishop had enrolled at Christopher Dock for his senior year and was in two of my classes. In my "Art of Clear Thinking" he brightened my day as one of my most cooperative and productive students, but in the bowling class his reluctant participation led to a sorry final grade of D+. I remembered him as a solid kid who played a mean electric guitar, extolled the virtues of *MAD* and embellished his notebook with cartoon figures. Little did I know that four years later he would join our faculty and kindle a flame that burns brightly to this present day.

Our relationship was enhanced when he began occupation of the classroom across the hall. We taught side by side with open doors as we challenged each other to greater heights. At my retirement reception in my heart-felt appreciation I stated, "When I started to feel weary like the old horse in the harness, your extra energy as a frisky colt, motivated me to give the load a stronger tug." There were times when he would scamper into my room where I was teaching with an idea or artifact to help clinch the moment and there were times when I shouted across the hall while he was teaching if I felt I had something critical to offer.

I developed a strong admiration for Eric as a model teacher. Much of his success was a result of his versatility, level of commitment, and boundless energy. But underneath it all was his vast awareness of the stuff that mattered to kids, along with his uncanny ability to connect with his students where they were, thereby making his efforts meaningful for the here and now. His rousing performances did not intimidate me, but I will concede to jealousy when I count the number of English majors his department, with the additional strength brought by CD alumnae Gretchen Miller McTavish (1973) and Bronwyn Mininger Histand (1981), has produced, compared to those who entered the history or social studies field.

To Schoolmaster Dock singing was a very vital element in school life. As the first music instructor and choir director at Christopher Dock High School, Hiram Hershey succeeded in establishing a strong vocal music tradition that has become one of the school's most cherished attributes. In 1967, while on the staff at Iowa Mennonite School, Ralph Alderfer of the CD Class of 1958 joined the CD faculty. For eighteen years he gave the school's music program a big boost. Since I was impressed with his strong leadership and had many fond memories of great quartet experiences I was surprised and disappointed when in 1986 he walked away from teaching and devoted full time to his house painting business.

1997 Faculty Quartet
Left to right: Steve Smucker, Eldon
Miller, Rodney Derstine, Duane Kauffman

Though Ralph's departure was keenly felt, CD music did not miss a beat. After teaching at Western Mennonite, Rodney Derstine from the Class of 1970 came home and for the last seventeen years has provided yeoman service. Rod's humor and down-to-earth manner endeared him to his students, but when it was time to get down to work he managed to inspire them to new heights. I enjoyed talking baseball with him and will long remember quartet moments, especially the Church and Synagogue Librarian Association banquets at Haverford and King of Prussia.

Two alumni Tims are worthy of comment. Tim Ehst from the Class of 1971 was one of the most assertive Campus Senate presidents with whom I served. He also was one of the school's most aggressive and talented basketball players as well. In the fall of 1978, after serving at Iowa Mennonite, he became part of the CD faculty. Under his direction the Physical Education Department took on a new look and as Athletic Director a broad interscholastic program was developed. Though usually a calm and casual kind of person, I was amazed at his metamorphosis as an intense basketball coach. At times he became so animated it threatened his health. Whether in faculty meeting, chapel presentation, team meeting, or personal conversation, I always appreciated his willingness to share details about his own faith journey in his striving for an even deeper level of spirituality.

The other Tim alumnus was Swartz from the Class of 1973. My memories of him as a student are vague but I remember him well as a member of the 1972 baseball team that I helped to coach. Though his role was pinch-hitting and mop-up pitching, I was impressed by his knowledge of the game and his willingness to help in any way possible. After graduation we kept in touch as we competed in the Knights of Menno Rotisserie Baseball League. For a decade his Swartz (Black) Sox and my Hackers dominated the competition as one or the other took home most of the trophies. At the time he accepted the 1999 call to become CD's art instructor he was a freelance artist who specialized in baseball related themes in oil paintings. (I have had the good fortune of obtaining a few which adorn the walls of my recreation room.) Though untrained and inexperienced as a teacher, he made steady progress as he gave the Art Department his own touch. As he worked in informal settings with his students, he found opportunities to not only spur them to utilize their creativity, but also to challenge them to be all that they could be in every respect.

In 1973 Eldon Miller brought his coal-black Afro and stage experience to CD. In the early years he taught Dramatic Arts and Short Story in addition to the Spanish classes. It seems that the stress of teaching soon got to him because within two years, his hair began to show some white streaks and by the time of my retirement thirty years later, his hair was even whiter than mine.

I'm sure he holds the school record for advising a particular club for the longest period of time. His A-V Club, though largely unappreciated, working behind the scenes, contributed an invaluable service. He was also on call to install a new projector bulb and provide valuable maintenance for many kinds of equipment. As coordinator of the Mexican Travel Experience his efforts contributed to more social studies learning in a few days than my teaching could provide in many weeks of classroom instruction. My memories of his melodious first tenor in our faculty quartet will long remain.

As I handed over the reins to colleague Ronald Hertzler I could move on in confidence that the CD Social Studies Department was in good hands. For sixteen years I enjoyed teaching with him. We were on the same wavelength and our styles were similar. I remember a few times when there was a question of who was the more animated, the teacher in D2 or the one in D3. After twelve years of teaching Ron surprised me by answering the summons to take on the role of Assistant Principal for the 1988–'89 school year. Though he did a commendable job, even serving as Acting Principal in 1997–'98, I was glad to see him return to full time teaching again in 1999. I've always envied his ability to eat heartily and still retain a slim figure. In fact, I once characterized him as "a lot of hotdog, but no buns." As a brother at Perkasie Mennonite I have been the recipient of his contributions in leadership and teaching there as well.

My personal memories of high school math have created such an aversion I cannot fathom why anyone would want to teach that subject. Yet Jerry Yoder has flourished in that capacity since 1974. Having him on the CD faculty has been quite helpful to me. In our growing up years we were both from the same community and had much in common. Since our backgrounds caused us to view things in much the same way, we have had many meaningful conversations. Our musical interests are very similar and I have thoroughly enjoyed the times we picked and sang together.

I have watched with interest as Martin Wiens has taken hold of the Assistant Principal position. He approached it cautiously, yet confidently. For him CD was not only a different kind of school, but he also found himself in a different type of Mennonite setting in a different part of the country. I have been intrigued by his approach to student discipline. There's something about it that gets results, but I don't fully comprehend it. It seems he has mastered the art of presenting a friendly, yet dignified image and his impact on students has grown out of hours of listening and cultivating solid relationships. During the last four years I have been the victim of ruthless ribbing. All this is due to the fact that in the great cycle of things his San Francisco Giants have completely dominated my Los Angeles Dodgers. Coming down the stretch he engaged in numerous light-hearted attempts to talk me out of retirement. I took it as a compliment and greatly appreciated his feedback and words of affirmation.

For a number of years Kathryn Hunsberger and I worked together as advisors for the Campus Senate. I was impressed with her careful attention to details and her willingness to support students by working side by side with them on various projects. Even more, I developed great respect for her as she provided special instruction and contributed mightily as part of the team in the Guidance Office. I have seen her patience and caring efforts pay big dividends in the lives of many students.

A few words yet about Ken Kabakjian who in 2003–2004 is enjoying a much deserved sabbatical leave. His role as facilitator for the ninth grade off-campus orientation-mixer has been significant in getting freshmen off to a good start. As Guidance Counselor he has not only done a yeoman job in academic advisement, but has helped to change the lives of students as he has hung in with them and provided them and their parents with unflagging support during tough times. His rapport with students has been enhanced by his upbeat style and sense of humor as shown by his performances as a juggler and a jester. I am deeply grateful for a number of meaningful videos he prepared to provide me with many fond memories of my CD experience.

I have heard many sordid tales of poor morale, individualism, and inter-clique rivalry found on a typical high school faculty. I can't imagine any teaching faculty anywhere that has functioned as much like a Christian community as the one with which I have been associated with for forty-five years. It has truly been both a joy and a blessing to have been part of the Christopher Dock faculty team.

19. OBSERVING AND RESPONDING TO CHANGE

The recent success of the girls' field hockey, boys' soccer, and boys' volleyball teams have created a frenzy that involved not only the student body, but alumni, parents, congregations, and community folks. The Pioneers put Christopher Dock Mennonite High School on the map as they traveled afar—even beyond the broad Susquehanna—to participate in tournament play. Players and coaches received statewide recognition. The school has invested in state-of-the-art athletic facilities that provide the very best for the players and are considered so superior that it is hard to keep up with the rental demands. Those associated with the school in its earliest years could never have even dreamed of something like this.

In 1955 the Board of Trustees went on record stating, "We believe competitive sports are wrong." It is not surprising, therefore, that when I came to CD in 1958 the athletic program was minimal. With the exception of two basketball games in 1961 and 1962, the competition for the first decade was strictly in-house. There was an extensive intramural program for boys in softball, volleyball, basketball and touch or flag football. Girls had volleyball and basketball from which to choose. Competition was usually class based but sometimes make-up teams played as well. Needless-to-say, I found myself involved in quite a bit of coaching and officiating. Until 1971 a highlight of the school year was the afternoon phase of Spring Day that was devoted to various track and field events. During the first ten years a tradition existed in which the senior boys played a team of alumni in a game in the packed gym during the Christmas vacation. In a preliminary game the faculty played a team of non-senior all-stars. The team of Hershey, Reinford, Kauffman, Detweiler, and Hess (later Hartzler) held our own quite well. I was not a star, but an article in the *Dockument* noted one occasion when I managed 16 points.

In 1964 the new gymnasium was completed and an inter-scholastic boy's basketball program soon developed. It started cautiously with a limited schedule with the Pioneers wearing rather conservative attire. The first two years, wearing white T-shirts and long trousers, they played eight games with Mennonite teams and two with Delco Christian, winning two of the events. The following year they played several Mennonite schools as they wore knickers and pulled on green jerseys over their white T-shirts. The next step was joining the Keystone Conference made up mostly of Protestant schools and several other private prep academies. By now shorts had replaced the knickers, but the white T-shirt was still under the jerseys. In 1975 CD joined a Catholic league that changed its name when we joined. By now the boys had gone all the way by discarding the white T-shirt and exposed themselves in sleeveless jerseys and shorts. Eventually our school landed in the Bicentennial League where one of the competing teams was even a military academy.

In the meantime the number of activities increased. In 1967–'68 a girls' basketball team was formed. A year later boys' soccer made its debut. The following year the girls' field hockey program was inaugurated. In 1972 the boys' baseball team in its first year brought home the school's first championship trophy. In 1973 girls' softball was started. Along the way tentative participation in tennis and track and field competition also occurred.

By the mid-eighties the athletic program was in full swing and it could be said that over half the students were involved in at least one sport at some point during the year. A girls' volleyball program was begun and tennis competition was provided for both sexes. The track and field events were stepped up. Boys' volleyball finally emerged and then a golf team even hit the links.

Another area in which we have come a long way is the utilization of classroom technology. When I arrived on the CD scene, we had not yet moved into the age of projected visuals. However I had a collection of LP records narrated by Edward R. Murrow entitled *I Can Hear it Now* in which students could hear the actual voices of Calvin Coolidge and Will Rodgers as well as listen to the frenzied description of the Hindenburg Disaster, an account of another Babe Ruth home run or listen to Roosevelt's "Day of Infamy" speech.

Then came the filmstrip projector. The first one required manual advancing while reading from a script. The second one had an LP record and the film was manually advanced after a beep. The next one had a record with an inaudible beep that moved the filmstrip ahead automatically. Finally an audiocassette replaced the record making the set less clumsy. By the late sixties motion picture projectors were available and by the seventies films could be obtained at the county's Intermediate Unit office. In my case I found threading and trouble-shooting these projectors to be a challenge I never completely mastered. When the school bought self-threading models things were less complicated but their rate of malfunctioning seemed high.

Then came the rolling carts with the VCR and monitor. This was a great step forward but I remember many frustrating occasions when I had planned to show a video only to have to do last minute scurrying to find the available equipment. Of course we are now in the day of mounted VCR/DVD and monitor units and computerization has brought us into the power point era.

In the 1970s the overhead projector made its appearance and soon became an indispensable medium in classroom instruction. It was a wonderful contraption that allowed projection of colored transparencies. It also provided the means to have my writing projected while facing the class.

Without a doubt this type of technology has greatly enhanced classroom instruction. Our school administrators should be commended for recognizing its potential and allocating sufficient funds to make it possible. These innovations made teaching more fun and in some ways easier, but it was sometimes tempting to use them as a crutch or a last minute cover-up for a poorly planned lesson.

Though the recent journey into digitalization has curbed the trend, I depleted a forest of trees with all the sheets of paper I used on the job. I can't imagine trying to teach without paper for tests, reviews, worksheets, maps, outlines, and listings of expectations. When I arrived the school had advanced to using a ditto machine. A master copy was typed or printed on a specially prepared form. This spirit master was then placed on a rotating drum of the hand-cranked device from which an alcohol-based liquid would seep and the result was a final copy with purple print. Special masters were available for other colors. Fixing typing errors was quite complicated necessitating scraping with a sharp instrument and inserting a strip of another master ditto into the typewriter while retyping. This was the standard procedure used until the late '80s. At that point a RISO machine was acquired that turned out large quantities of black print and finally under Business Manager Jeff Ambrose's leadership, photocopy machines were acquired with mind-boggling multiple features.

Though cramped for practice time and space, under the direction of violin virtuoso Stanley Yoder, Christopher Dock High has developed an outstanding instrumental program. Each year more and more students have been chosen for district and regional performances. Though today's jazz band and orchestra are the school's pride and joy, the journey to this point has been long and challenging.

When I began to teach at CD, all musical instruments were banned. In an attempt to preserve the highly valued a cappella singing tradition, the original school constitution flatly asserted, "Musical instruments shall not be a part of the school's equipment, nor be used on the premises. All recorders and record players used as a part of instruction in the school shall be under the supervision of the Administrative Committee."

Some interesting scenarios developed because of this policy. I remember one that had a particularly ironic twist. The choir at times would walk out the lane together to the home of the Board President Paul Clemens and use his piano to help them learn the music. On other occasions Hiram Hershey would have someone record the piano accompaniment and play it while the choir rehearsed.

Many of the students were accomplished musicians. Some had gone to public schools and taken lessons there. Quite a few had pianos in their homes. In fact the father of several students sold pianos, guitars, and accordions and had a staff that provided instruction. For the senior retreat at Camp Swatara students brought and played their guitars, violins, and accordions and a regular highlight was gathering around the piano for singing.

Musical instruments on the CD campus sneaked in through the back door. A number of claims are made for the appearance of the first piano. All I know is that I was personally involved in an early one as advisor to the Class of 1962. In the May 1961 Junior-Senior Banquet, Clemmer Music delivered a piano to the school for our use. Though I remember time being spent in leveling it, I don't recall its being played during the performance. I suspect a few notes were struck and it was probably more than a mere part of the décor.

After a Board appointed task force released the findings of a poll of the school's constituency, the Franconia Conference leadership approved a constitutional revision allowing tape recorders and instruments "as long as the practices did not endanger unaccompanied singing." By the spring of 1966 a new upright piano was on the auditorium stage thanks to the gift bestowed by the Class of 1966.

When I arrived in 1958 the center of activity was the converted dairy barn known as Grebel Hall. A new wing had just been completed that summer. The ground floor consisted of the cafeteria, boys' and girls' showers and locker rooms, furnace room, and two classrooms. The second level had two classrooms, auditorium with a raised stage and the gymnasium. The gym was so small that it had no provision for spectators and successful shots from half-court were not uncommon. Folding partitions that opened into the gym and adjacent classrooms could enlarge the auditorium.

An old carriage building included two science labs and on the top floor the home economics suite was located. The grand, three-storied mansion, simply called the "Ad Building," housed administrative offices and library on the first floor with classrooms on the second. Classes were not held on the third floor but a room there was used as a photography darkroom, and another was reserved for an infirmary that later was designated the prayer room.

Most of the land around the buildings was open space. Finishing touches were being made to the recently constructed pond in 1958. Fields that were farmed lay on two sides of Grebel Hall. Below the "Ad Building" was a meadow with a meandering stream. Once used for pasture, it was now overgrown with saplings, thickets of overgrown shrubs, and clusters of briars and brambles. Remains of a rail fence were still standing in some places. In the summer of 1959 I helped others open things up as we tore down the fence, cut off the blackberry bushes, sumac, and elderberries, and trimmed back the undisciplined lilacs.

Then there was the well and all the legends surrounding it! Today a discerning eye can detect a depression next to a large pine tree in the grass island in the main driveway circle. This is the old hand-dug, stone-lined well. By the time I joined the faculty, it had been filled with refuse and covered with a heavy sheet of metal. During later landscaping it was filled in completely and several trees were planted next to it. According to local folklore, the well was an entrance to a tunnel that was used for hiding slaves on the Underground Railroad. The tunnel tales have several variations. Some claim it connected to the basement of the mansion. Another variation had it running to the neighboring farm. In the first issue of the school newspaper an interview was reviewed in which a local codger claimed it went all the way to the Sumneytown Pike. Despite all the hearsay, I am not aware of any serious excavation efforts in an attempt to get to the bottom of the well saga.

During my years at CD I have seen the property become a campus that qualifies as one of the region's most impressive sites. Though the Board of Trustees deserves commendation for its careful planning and execution, much of the credit belongs to science and art teacher Roland Yoder whose ideas and efforts managed to balance the functional and aesthetic and Claude Groff who made maintenance and beautification of the campus his retirement vocation.

In the 1963–'64 school year a much-needed multi-purpose building—later called Clemens Center—was completed which provided a new cafeteria, auditorium, and gymnasium. This allowed for Grebel Hall renovations that brought the library there and made possible the addition of more classrooms. I remember my feelings of awe when I first saw the new gym. It seemed as huge as the Farm Show Building Arena. I was chief advisor to the class that had the Pioneer logo proudly painted on the magnificent hardwood floor. It never dawned on me that a day would come when this impressive facility would be scorned much like its predecessor.

1978 saw another great leap forward in campus growth. An annex was made to Clemens Center with created classroom space with particular attention given to music and physical education needs. Even more significant was the erection of a new classroom building named Dielman Hall in honor of one of Schoolmaster Dock's dear friends, Dielman Kolb. Due to my seniority I was allowed to "pull rank" in choosing my room so I selected the one at the far end of the hall. I often applauded my choice since it gave me many great opportunities to look out the window and see birds at the feeder and enjoy the daffodils that I had planted on the bank. I remember the excitement of moving day when classes were suspended and students carried materials from my room in G4 to my new classroom in D3. Unfortunately, two students carelessly dropped one of my file drawers denting the corner and spilling the contents.

Nothing could be compared to the 5.6 million dollar 1995–'96 effort that culminated in Longacre Center. Now there was a double gymnasium with an indoor track, a state-of-the-art fitness center, student commons, 200-seat "audion", and four large classrooms. This complex has proved to be a tremendous asset to

1995 Symbolic ground-breaking for Longacre Center
Left to right: Gerald Benner, Donna Weaver, Henry Longacre, Gail and Sandy Alderfer, Gerry Moore, Henry Rosenberger, Jerry Moore, Duane Kauffman, Lee Delp

the school and community, but I must admit it overwhelms me and it seems like an undeserved luxury.

But it still wasn't finished. In 2001–'02 another two million dollars were spent renovating the lower level of the Clemens Center Annex for more classrooms. An additional part of the project was the installation of a lighted track and playing field with artificial turf. Contiguous sites were also provided for other types of sporting events and it was topped off with bleachers and a multi-purpose building.

I have also observed significant changes in the student population. In 1958, 179 students were enrolled. Within two decades, the size had doubled and by 1980 it would reach a figure of 420. In observing this trend my feelings are mixed. Naturally I was enthused to be part of a vital and growing institution. It was good to have opportunities to reach out to a greater number of Mennonite youth and to sense a stronger support from local Mennonite congregations. Yet there were times when I had nostalgic moments when I missed the smaller, more intimate, school family that could be stuffed into the small auditorium for chapel, crammed into the gym for an all-school social, or packed into a few cars for an off-campus "school day out."

How many times have I heard the question, "How are students different from when you first started to teach?" I usually hesitate to answer because by the tone I can tell it's a loaded one. It seems they expect me to berate youth for what they perceive to be their disrespect, lack of motivation or self-centeredness. I don't go there! I usually stall them by saying, "The adolescent creature has not changed. They assume they are more enlightened and will constantly push the limits to 'test their wings.'" That said, it is certainly true that I have seen big changes in how they look, what they patronize, and where they go.

Today a glance at a typical CD student does not reveal anything that would set that person apart from students in any other school. I have seen dress code revisions necessitated by the vanishing devotional covering, unconventional hairstyles, rising hemlines, falling necklines, low-slung trousers, exposed midriffs, and bejeweled body piercing. Christopher Dock students go to the same concerts and visit the same music stores as other youth. They read the same magazines and books, and watch the same television programs. They can be found in the same theaters, video arcades, discotheques, malls, and amusement parks as they mingle with the general youth population.

Yes, today's students at Christopher Dock are worldlier than those of earlier days. Since the school's founders and early supporters hoped for a place that would provide a shelter from worldly influences, they would be greatly disturbed by what they would see.

As a CD teacher I was aware of the increased use and blasé attitude about drugs and alcohol. I have been shocked and disappointed by the pregnancies and rumors of sexual promiscuity. At times I have been embarrassed when we have graduated students who have not measured up to school's level of expectations.

But, there's the rest of the story! The patterns and priorities of the faculty and parents have also kept pace with the larger society. The Mennonite Church no longer emphasizes external "nonconformity to the world." In the final analysis, all that today's students are doing is reflecting the values of the adult community. I am not convinced that today's youth are less spiritual than their predecessors. In recent years I have become impressed with their involvement in service projects. Their level of spiritual maturity and their freedom to dialogue about their faith journey have challenged me.

I believe that a higher percentage of today's students are academically motivated. In the late 50s a group would start out together as freshmen, but by the time of their senior year ten per cent would have dropped out. Admittedly there was often a core that was strongly committed academically, but the proportion that lacked incentive was greater than today.

Today's students are a product of urbanization. Those of yesterday represented a more rural and agricultural society. 60%

came from farms. I can still remember some boys who came to school smelling like the stable. Some fell asleep because they were up at 5:00 AM milking the cows. Some with potential in drama or athletics could not participate because they had chores to do at home.

Though today's students may be more urbane and cosmopolitan, I miss the farm values of cooperation and community that have been pushed aside by the individualism of the urban society.

20. FINDING THE BALANCE

Your family needs you. The church calls. Your body and spirit crave rest and renewal. How do you juggle these competing loyalties? I lived with constant tension because I never found a satisfactory solution. Though never completely incapacitated, trying to handle the pressure of meeting expectations of others and myself, and dealing with the guilt of falling short of the mark, took its toll.

I never developed a standardized daily or weekly schedule that allocated a block of time for each activity. My life seemed to require more flexibility, since there were particular days or weeks when the needs in a certain realm were greater than in others.

I tended to see teaching as my first priority and interpreted other demands as intrusions. However, that often left me wondering if that preoccupation meant I was giving other obligations short shrift.

For me teaching was not just another eight-hour day or forty-hour week job. Counting time on the road, at school, and preparation at home, my time calculated to between eleven and twelve hours per weekday. In some ways school became almost an obsession. If I managed to find some extra time, there was always some school-related activity that could easily consume it. I realize that I put a lot more time in class preparation and projects than most. Teaching is often perceived to be a God-given gift. That may be true, but in my case the gift did not come already assembled, polished and ready for use. Nor were instructions enclosed. I had to work hard to develop the level of competency that not only would meet the standards of others, but my own, as well. I put considerable pressure on myself since my expectations were so high. Sometimes I would hear people say, "You've been teaching so long that it must be pretty easy by now." Though repetition did help in mastery of basic content, I was never satisfied and always tried to find ways to improve my teaching. In the social studies field the world constantly changed and a new angle or application just might be the clincher. If you show me a veteran teacher that doesn't devote as much time and effort as was given earlier, I will show you a slacker!

Teachers with children have my sympathy and admiration. I don't see how they manage since the demands of parenting dare not be minimized. Naomi and I had no children, but still found it hard to find much time for each other. If I had been involved in raising a family, my commitment to teaching in terms of time and energy would most certainly have been less.

How do you say no to your church? At one point I kept my congregational involvement to a minimum. I rationalized that my school was also my church. I reasoned that my faculty brothers and sisters were my Christian fellowship and three chapels each week provided opportunities for worship and spiritual nourishment. This rationale never satisfied my church family and I was never comfortable with it myself.

CD teachers felt some pressure from the school to be involved in a local congregation. Hopefully this was done to enhance the teacher's spiritual growth or as a resource the school had to share. But, it felt somewhat like a public relations ploy to reach out to parents and youth who would be potential applicants for admission.

In time I developed a deep love for my congregation and found fulfillment in participation. I wanted to offer my gifts for the mission of the church. Yet at times it seemed like the congregation's appetite for my services was insatiable and I was in danger of being swallowed up. I resented the assumption "that said since you have the gift to teach, we should always be able to count on you for Bible school or Sunday school. As I allowed myself to be used more and more, I found myself serving in demanding roles such as chairing the Board of Elders, Church Council, or Gifts Discernment Committee. These responsibilities were not only time consuming, but energy sapping as well. There were Wednesday nights when after facilitating an emotional discernment meeting, I had trouble falling asleep.

I also heard other voices such as that of the Mennonites of Eastern Pennsylvania. For over thirty years I served on their Board of Trustees and assisted as a volunteer at the Heritage Center. Every October I helped set up for the annual Apple Butter Frolic and took my place demonstrating cider making.

Making cider at the 1996 Apple Butter Frolic, Abner Schlabach on the left.

This was natural for me with my interest and knowledge about local Mennonite history. It was enriching and a nice change-of-pace, but it did take time and energy.

Though my commitments to school, church, and the Historians was high and my roles demanding, and though the pressure of one responsibility made it hard to "pull my weight" in another, I would not have wanted it any other way. My level of participation was a result of my own choices. I could have said "no" more often. Nobody compelled me to go to school an hour early each morning, or to agree to teach Sunday school, or to be a Thursday evening volunteer in the Historical Library. I did these things because I felt needed and I received a sense of ful-fillment and satisfaction in return.

There were other enjoyable activities that helped to bring a necessary balance by providing relaxation and renewal. My eleven or twelve hour school days had spaces. The fifty minutes on the road was not wasted time. I took the scenic route and lis-tened to KYW or audiocassettes on the way. When I arrived I had time to have a brief devotional and read the *North Penn Reporter* while I drank a tasty cup of "Constant Comment" tea. And in all honesty, some of the evening paper checking was done to the accompaniment of a radio broadcast of a baseball or bas-ketball game.

Also in maintaining my property at home, there were tasks to be carried out. It was work, but a check with my neighbors would reveal that I was usually singing or whistling while I was mowing the lawn, raking the leaves, or weeding the flowerbeds.

Naomi and I enjoyed our dinners out on Friday evenings and our occasional visits to flea markets and antique shops as we added to our Stangl starflower, Boscal peanut butter tumbler, or Sebastian figurine collections. We found pleasure in drives to see the flowering dogwoods at Valley Forge or the brilliant autumn foliage in the Hosensack Valley. Our walks in Nockamixon and Tyler state parks or on the Delaware Canal towpath brought great delight.

I have had and still have my hobbies. Once I collected coins and stereographic cards but I have put them aside. I had several hives of bees that provided fascination and honey until wiped out by the wax moths. I also took advantage of the close proximity to Philadelphia where I enjoyed a couple of baseball games a year. I've been left with some interesting memories of these occasions. Whenever I meet alumni Jim or Henry they always remind me of the time I took several students to a game and we came home reeking of the odor of beer. I don't remember all the details, but it was on our clothing, and not on our breath. On another occasion a half-dozen CD faculty men were at old Connie Mack Stadium for the "Grand Finale." Like the others, I ended up dismantling my seat and taking home one of the slats as a souvenir. At this point my biggest pastime is my orchard of antique apples. My grandfather was known for his apples and apple butter and an old map of my great grandfather's orchard of over a hundred years ago stimulated my interest. Some of the old varieties like Smokehouse, Northern Spy, or Grimes Golden are still hard to beat, but others are now long forgotten because of their poor taste or susceptibility to disease. Throughout the years, thanks to the help of my good friend Larry Godshall, the maintenance supervisor at CD, some good cider has been delivered to CD personnel.

My most satisfying diversions have been those involving my teaching colleagues. For nine years, five or six of us were involved in a rotisserie baseball league. The Sunday afternoons closest to the opening of the regular baseball season were exciting times as we drafted our players and engaged in transaction. For three years I anchored the CD bowling team in the Town and Country Industrial League. I'll long remember Wilbur Leidig's side-arm delivery and the 212 Roland Yoder bowled in his first game as a substitute. Of all the sports in which I have participated, bowling would take first place. I looked forward to the occasions when Dick Lichty and Gerald Benner and I would bowl at the Lansdale Town and Country Lanes regularly after school. I enjoyed bowling in the handicap league at Quaker Lanes where I held my own quite well with my high series a 647 and an average in the 170s. The time came when bowling was something I had to let go. Today I do not miss it and I haven't touched my bowling ball for over twelve years. Perhaps in retirement this is one thing I will pick up again.

I have always been interested in music. I especially enjoy singing Scottish and Appalachian ballads and singing in male choirs and quartets. I like a variety of genres ranging from classical to folk. For a number of years, I was a member of the Franconia and Lancaster Choral Singers. It was a significant commitment that called for learning challenging music and rehearsals every Tuesday evenings in season. When my church involvement increased, this was the one major activity I dropped. For the last decade I have listened to people who scolded me for not using the singing gift God gave me as much as I should. Since my retirement from CD I am back in the Franconia and Lancaster Choral Singers fold again.

In thinking about balancing my various activities I have gained some perspective by reminding myself that I have not been called to be a teacher or a church elder, but rather, I am called to serve God in whatever way I can to the best of my ability. However, the reality still remains. I have tough choices to make.

21. RELUCTANT SUBMISSION

When Assistant Principal Ronald Hertzler was on his 1996–'97 sabbatical leave he served as Interim Principal at Penn View Christian, CD's primary feeder school. When he returned the following year as Acting Principal at CD he talked about the Penn View sixth grade class. He went on to say that there was a core of boys that would likely require alternative approaches to learning and assessment. I remember thinking to myself, "Bring them on. I accept the challenge. I'll just have to try harder and do better."

Sure enough, the time came when the "unscholarly dozen" arrived. Ron was right. They didn't fit the mold. Since I had no freshmen in classes, I was spared. However, I heard the sorry tales of frustration from teachers who were at their wits' end in knowing how to deal with them. My attitude was, "give them to me and we'll see." The following year they were all in my tenth grade U.S. History classes. To say they were not academically motivated was an understatement. They bucked the system and were almost defiant as they dared me to try to get them interested in history. They acted as though they were unjustly incarcerated. Their attention drifted during class activities. They refused to hand in assignments and because they didn't study, they consistently failed quizzes and tests.

During the first semester they were distributed nicely among my five sections. In each case a solid motivated majority set a good tone so classroom management was not a problem. I stayed with the principle, "if you don't produce, you will not get credit." In this case that consequence didn't have much of an impact. To receive an F didn't seem to faze them. The enticement of a CD diploma or visions of college beyond had no appeal. But by the end of the semester I had managed to cajole them so that only two ended up with failing grades. In response to a plan designed by the Guidance Office in consultation with parents, two were given special consideration and received passing marks based on an individualized educational program.

Then came semester two. When I received my class lists, I almost went into shock. My first period class had only eleven students, but six were of the "awful dozen." There were two academically gifted, highly motivated girls and one other "studious boy." After the first meeting of the class I came to the point where I saw no option but to do something drastic. The first move was to transfer the two exceptional students to one of my other sections of the class. The "studious boy" wanted to stay. I then had one of the "dozen" moved from another section into the first period class.

That gave me a class of ten. Seven were of the "dozen," two with individualized educational programs and the "studious boy." Another boy was marginal and would go with the flow. To make things more interesting, there was one glamorous girl who thoroughly relished her queenly role.

In managing the class I permitted a more informal style. Since there were only ten and they all sat in a small semi-circle according to my plan, control wasn't much of a problem. I brought myself closer to their level by sitting while I led the discussions. Instead of adhering to the textbook I used a variety of videos depending heavily on Haley's *Roots*, Ken Burns' *Civil War* and *The West*, and a biography of Theodore Roosevelt. I distributed a set of questions for each 15 to 20 minute clip and then spent the remainder of the period discussing them. In my tests, I gave them options of doing short essays or the more traditional multiple-choice questions. In homework assignments they were given more alternatives and time in class to work under my supervision.

By the end of the course Tyler got his B while John, Ben D., Ben M., Jeremy, Greg, Seth, Luke, Rachel, and Josh mastered the content quite well and earned a passing grade. In the end both sides won. They won in the sense that they humbled me and brought me to the point of submission. Of course it was a conditional surrender in the sense that I did not capitulate completely. However, I did meet them more than halfway.

I also won because I gained their confidence when they saw I was on their side. I gained the ultimate victory by getting a good performance from them and a much healthier attitude. I received written and verbal comments from a number of the students saying it was their favorite course and I got gestures of appreciation from a number of parents.

In the final analysis it proved that "an old dog can learn new tricks." It seemed to confirm the idea that methodology and content are secondary and what really counts the most, is for the student to feel the warmth of a teacher's caring heart. I also wonder how much these students had been damaged at some point when they saw themselves as failures and gave up. I say this in light of some conversations I had with parents who constantly reminded me of their learning difficulties and gave me advice about the need to lower my expectations.

Last year (2002–2003) I had a difficult situation that called for a similar response. One of the things I have always dreaded was the extra pressure of having seniors during the last nine weeks in a course they had to pass in order to meet graduation requirements. Though I had developed a semi-thick hide, I didn't want to be the culprit that prevented that triumphant march across the stage. It happened several times and the memories still linger.

Ancient Greece and Rome was the most difficult class I taught and six or eight seniors needing it for graduation got off to a very slow start. At the halfway mark Colleen and Austin were far behind and it soon became apparent that mathematically they were doomed and there was no way for them to get their diplomas with the other students. It would mean a remedial summer program and a belated diploma.

At that point I checked with the Guidance Office and discovered they both had a study hall during my free period. I decided to give them a chance for a passing grade so I made them a proposition. Instead of going to study hall they were to report to my classroom where I would give them individualized assignments and tutoring. They were told to let me know in advance if they would not be able to come. It was understood they were expected to cooperate fully and there would be no tolerance for any deviation.

Admittedly, I did not have much hope. Austin was dealing with some very tough personal matters. He tended to be uncommunicative and at times surly. Colleen was in my advisor group and I just couldn't seem to relate to her. It didn't help that I had to occasionally nudge her to keep her awake in chapel. Toward the end of the year I felt like some progress was made when she talked a bit about her yoga experiences and said "hello" when I saw her at the restaurant.

In the end both Austin and Colleen came through in fine style and I could pass them with a clear conscience and a feeling of deep satisfaction. Since I felt like I had given them a gift that made their graduation possible, my pride was wounded when neither mentioned me in their senior presentation. (This was a reflection on me because I should have understood they would not talk about the situation in front of their peers and friends.) However, after the Commencement events I received a hug and words of appreciation from Austin and his parents were profuse in their praise. And Colleen surprised me and almost brought me to tears by asking me to pose with her while her parents took our picture. What really topped it off happened at my retirement reception. Who were the first to arrive? None other than Colleen and her parents! These rewards for going the "extra mile," far outweighed the extra work and inconvenience entailed.

22. IF I COULD DO IT OVER AGAIN

In looking back it is not difficult to identify certain decisions or actions that call up unpleasant memories or feelings of dissatisfaction. I find myself saying, "If I only had another chance, I would do things differently." Below, I will share some of my regrets. If I could do it over again I would:

1. **Attend more athletic events.**
   Though I thoroughly enjoyed athletic competition, my support as a cheering spectator was minimal. I often had good intentions, but at the last minute other priorities won out. On the occasions when I did attend I was well aware of how much it meant to the students, particularly the cheerleaders and players. Once when I attended an afternoon girls' softball game I felt like a distraction because my presence seemed more important than the game itself.

2. **Never use corporal punishment.**
   In the early days of my teaching, it was not uncommon for a teacher to resort to physical punishment. In my case there were four regrettable episodes. In three, it was an impulsive lashing out, and only one was the result of a deliberate plan. Two occurred in the context of phys-ed when I slapped boys in the facial area. In one of these, I knocked the student's eyeglasses to the floor. Both were a result of losing control in exasperation from putting up with too much sassing. Eddie was a unique

character who often wore a necktie to school and in one of our clashes I grabbed his tie and gave it a good yank. The most spectacular event was the one that was not a mere impulse. Dave seemed to chatter all the time. I had him sitting in a front desk and I walked up so I was standing right beside him. When he started to babble once more I slapped his mouth. Unfortunately my aim was an inch too high and blood began to pour from his nose. At that point I said to a tall boy in the back of the room, "Mr. Brenneman, since your father is a doctor, you take this fellow to the bathroom and take care of him." I shakily continued to teach the hushed class, but at that point I resolved I would never lay a hand on another student.

3.   Offer more apologies.

In the events described above, I later approached three of the students I slapped and apologized and in two cases I called the parents and admitted my poor judgment. For me, recognizing my mistake and offering an apology was an extremely difficult thing to do. On a number of occasions I apologized to a class for a sub-par performance or a bad test or assignment. It was fairly easy to offer this kind of generic apology, but it was much harder to tell a student, "What I did was wrong. I'm sorry. Will you forgive me?" There was an incident when Steve came to me after class. He was obviously angry. He went on to tell me that he was hurt by what I had said in his absence the previous day. In taking the roll, and noting Steve was not in class again, I made a snide comment about it and suggested he didn't seem to be all that interested in graduating. After he confronted me, I realized what I had done and accompanied him to the empty faculty lounge where I admitted my fault and asked for forgiveness. I remember yet, his smile when he shook my hand as he said, "Sure." The times when I brought myself to ask for forgiveness, I felt the humility was well worth the internal cleansing and the restoration of a broken relationship.

4. Use less sarcasm.

Perhaps the use of sarcasm has its place in certain cases. Though it didn't happen frequently, this was one area where I mismanaged situations on too many occasions. It seemed like I merely replaced physical with verbal slaps. I cannot think of many cases where this tactic led to better conduct or an improved attitude. Even if the student was less disruptive in class, the act was often damaging in terms of relationships. Words are so volatile that at times I discovered I had hurt a student by what I said when that was the last thing I wanted to do.

5. Plan more field trips.

In my earlier years of teaching I took classes to the Classical History Museum of the campus of the University of Pennsylvania or to Valley Forge or other sites in the Bucks-Mont area. Though these were excellent learning experiences, I got away from the practice. One reason I backed off was the recognition of the impact field trips had on other classes. They also demanded considerable time and effort in terms of making the necessary arrangements. I should have taken better advantage of the rich heritage on our doorstep.

6. Be more active as a department chair.

In my role as department chair, I feel I was quite active in curriculum review and revision. I did an adequate job when it came to textbook selection and acquisition of resources. Though a number of social studies teachers also taught in other departments, I could have called more meetings and planned more group activities. My biggest neglect was in working with new teachers. I should have checked in with them more frequently and set up times to observe them and provide opportunities for them to watch me in action. These kinds of opportunities could have been followed by times of evaluation and plans for improvement.

**At the Lower Skippack Mennonite Church
Cemetery grave of Christopher Dock**

7. **Spend more time in the faculty lounge.**

I had a tendency to be reclusive and do my own thing. This was especially true after my migration to the far-away realm of C8 in the bowels of Clemens Center. Since I was out of the loop, I missed out on a lot more than I was aware. I'm sure my day could have been brightened by the jokes and light-hearted banter. I also could have sensed more of the team spirit and have been better informed about what was happening in the lives of my colleagues. It would also have given me a better feel for the pulse of campus life.

8. **Stay in touch with alumni.**

Schoolmaster Christopher Dock stayed in touch with his former students and wrote them letters admonishing them to remain true to the faith. But, this is another place where I have not measured up. Many opportunities for continuing friendships were lost because I failed to follow up with students after graduation. One of my more obvious shortcomings has been my reluctance to attend class reunions to which I have been invited. I am presently finding e-mail correspondence as a good way to stay in touch, but even so, I need to do better.

9. **Provide more alternative plans for learning and assessment.**

As I noted earlier, I have been very slow to make exceptions in dealing with learning disabilities or different styles of learning. I suppose much of this could be attributed to stubbornness on my part. Some of it was a suspicion of psychologists who had exonerating labels for what I perceived to be laziness or lack of self-discipline. In all honesty, I still suspect a few hide behind these diagnoses and slide by, giving far less than they could. However, within the last few years I have seen the use of different types of assignments and alternate kinds of assessment unlock something that frees some students for better performance and contributes toward building more self-esteem.

10. Be more open in sharing my personal spiritual pilgrimage

In chapel, classroom situations, and conversations, it was not hard to point out what the Bible said or to comment on what others believed. Though I benefited tremendously from the faith stories of others, I have kept my faith private and have always been uncomfortable talking about it. Actions speak louder than words, but I am sure I lost opportunities where allowing a glimpse into my spiritual life would have made a difference.

23. THE BONUS YEAR

In June 1999, after 38 years as an elementary public school teacher and librarian, my wife retired. At that point I spent much time contemplating my own approaching departure. Two years later would have been a logical time to leave since I would be reaching the big number 65. One thing I was determined to avoid was hanging on too long. I had perceived that to be the case with my colleague Harvey and I had seen it in baseball with Robin Roberts, Steve Carlton, and Don Sutton. I wanted to go out on top before my image was tarnished by mediocrity. Admittedly, my reasoning was self-serving and secondary to stepping aside for someone with fresh ideas and more energy.

Things were still going well in the classroom and we had just made some significant revisions in the social studies curriculum that I wanted to see take effect. As a result, I decided to postpone my social security days and continue on until the end of the 2001–'02 school year. I was at peace with the decision and "girded up my loins" for a good last year.

This 44th year turned out to be one of my most challenging. Coping with the "awful dozen" in my U.S. History class was a real test. Throughout the year I was often frustrated and it was not until it was nearly over, that I began to see things in a more positive light. At the same time new concepts were being introduced in long range planning that stretched me into an uneasy position. Discussions centered on things like curriculum mapping, co-construction of curriculum, and developing a non-traditional approach to a Middle States Association self study that included a plan for a student to reflect, articulate, and demonstrate core values. I did not oppose moving in this direction, but at the same time, I had a problem conjuring up enthusiastic support. I also found myself being pushed in the uncomfortable direction of greater utilization of computer technology. So, I took my decision to retire for granted and began to plan when I should send my letter of resignation to the Board of Trustees and how I would announce my plans to the student body.

But along the way, something unexpected happened. During the junior class Thanksgiving chapel I was called to the front of the auditorium while a short power point play on the then popular Master Card commercial was presented. It declared:

> **One minute of U.S. History Class** . . . . .19.5 cents
> **One period of U.S. History Class:** $7.80
> **One semester of U.S. History Class:** $702.00
> **Mr. Kauffman staying one more year:** . . . . . . .PRICELESS
> **There are some things that money can't buy.**
> **For everything else there's late retirement.**

The standing ovation that followed overwhelmed me. Then during the Christmas candy cane distribution I received over a dozen notes from the Class of 2003 that affirmed my teaching and pleaded with me to return for another year. Along the way Assistant Principal Wiens was playfully keeping the possibility alive by giving me student feedback along with comments of his own. In the meantime I was beginning to reconsider and brought the matter to my church small group. They also encouraged me to postpone my exit. Though my wife's preference was for me to follow through with my earlier decision, she made it clear it was entirely up to me.

In mid-March two things happened that clinched my reversal of plans. One day after students had been registering for the coming year's classes, Cailin came up to me beaming with excitement as she announced she had signed up for both Local History and Ancient Greece and Rome. I replied, "That's great, but I don't know who will be teaching them." Her pained, tearful expression as she turned and bolted, cut me deeply. The second thing made it final. I had planned to write my retirement letter for the Board of Trustees over the weekend, but that Friday Dave walked into my room and told me he had just informed the principal he would not be returning. This was a real shock since I had assumed he would be moving up to the position of department chair and I had confidence that things would be in capable hands. The timing and the implication of both full-time social studies teachers leaving at the same time did not seem to be in the best interest of the school. He had beaten me to the draw. This led me to the moment when at the beginning of a chapel service, I walked to the microphone and said, "One more year? (*Pause*) One more year!" and then walked to my seat to a thunderous applause.

An item in the April 9 issue of the *North Penn Reporter* made me feel like my decision was right. I was stunned when in a special feature honoring Alex for his soccer achievements, in response to the question, "Who is your role model?" he responded with, "Mr. Kauffman, my social studies teacher." Coming from him that was one of the greatest compliments I ever received.

When the 2002–'03 school year began I did not know what to expect. Though never articulated, a reason for my return was to see if I could improve on my previous year and go out on a more positive note. My tenth grade U.S. History classes were exceptionally good both semesters. But it was the Class of 2003 that kept me riding on a cloud throughout the year.

The attitude and cooperation of my advisor group was unbelievable. Their chapels conduct and participation was most exemplary. When they met in the special Tuesday and Thursday study hall in my room they were a model of quiet production.

During the year I had a dream come true when with the cooperation of seniors in my Local History class I finally taught a class in which I gave no tests, quizzes, or specific assignments. I provided a list of suggestions and depended entirely on student initiative. Janae, Kate, Katie, and Kristen made it work by setting the bar high with their level of commitment and I was pleased to give every student a well-deserved passing grade.

For making the year so memorable I would like to give special recognition to:

Cailin for her interest and intelligent analyses of history and current events and for her part in painting and presenting the large watercolor portrait of me.

Carl ("**Boomer**") for his great whimsical caricature painting.

"**Liz**" for her indirect, but significant, compliment she gave by the dismay displayed when she discovered she was not in my Ancient Greece and Rome class.

Rachel for her notes of appreciation and affirmation,

Bonnie for her hugs and good conversations and honoring me by composing and performing *A Force to be Reckoned With*. (See *Appendix*.)

Charity for sharing some of the best cookies I ever tasted.

Brian for his strong affirmation of the Social Studies Department and his decision to major in political science.

Aaron for leaving me nice paintings and sketches similar to those his father produced a generation before and for co-creating the watercolor portrait of me.

Andrew C. for asking me to be Santa and for his special interest in history even if he is obsessed with the military dimension.

Kara for being my chapel seatmate and making sure I had a hymnal to use.

**Participating in the 2002
Senior Christmas Chapel**

"Looks like Santa Claus, sounds like God"

Ashley for nominating me for *Who's Who Among American Teachers*.

Katie for her outstanding leadership in chapels and patience with me for my propensity to call her Kathy.

Eric for his excellent contributions to class discussion and an e-mail tag mrkauffmanismyfavoriteteacher@yahoo.com that was hard to ignore.

Miles Musselman presenting special shirt to Duane Kauffman after a May 2003 chapel presentation

Janae for her kind words during her senior presentation and my retirement reception.

Rob for the Thanksgiving power point presentation and cheerful assistance with my computer problems.

Kate for her leadership as Campus Senate secretary and her exuberant school spirit.

Kyle for his steady performance as Campus Senate president and our conversations about JWY, a mutual interest.

To receive a standing ovation is one of the greatest honors a person can receive. During this special year I was thrice blest in this manner. The first came after an old friend Jake Rittenhouse, who was in chapel as a conductor of a choir from Hesston College, led everybody in singing *Happy Birthday*. The second came after I participated in a May chapel facilitated by Eric Bishop in which I was recognized in a presentation by Miles during which I was given a Dodger baseball shirt with the name

Recognizing standing ovation after delivering 2003 commencement address

KAUFFMAN and a big 45 on the back. The third came after I was given an honorary CD diploma at the conclusion of my commencement address.

As it turned out, changing my mind and returning for one more year was one of the best decisions I ever made. It was the capstone to forty-five wonderful years.

With Seniors at 2003 Commencement
Left to right: Douglas Hackman, Andrew Moore, Kristen Souder, Ryan Detweiler, Kyle Yoder

24. THE BIG SEND-OFF

As the school year drew to a close there were a number of special occasions during which I was given special recognition. Though being treated as a celebrity made me uncomfortable, the expressions of gratitude and affirmation will be forever cherished.

After giving my commencement address I was surprised by the request to remain at the podium. After some kind words, Principal Elaine Moyer presented me with a Christopher Dock diploma. This was particularly interesting since in my concluding remarks I had pointed out I would be graduating too but would not be getting a diploma. The gesture had a special meaning since my dear friend Roland Yoder did the fraktur design.

Another big surprise was the discovery that the 2003 *Schul Andenken* honored me with a two-page feature entitled "45 Years in the Classroom: An Extraordinary Commitment to Mennonite Education." It included eight photos including four that showed my changing appearance as the years went by. Colleague Eric Bishop presented a three-paragraph tribute. Another section, labeled "Kauffman Klassics," noted some of my unique verbal expressions. Space was devoted to "Words from the Whipper-snappers" in which six students honored me with personal words of appreciation. (Though I'm not quite sure what Bonnie meant when she said, I "sang like a thundercloud," I'll take that as a compliment too.)

At the end of the school year there is a tradition of an annual luncheon for the entire CD staff during which persons are honored

Receiving honorary diploma from Principal Elaine Moyer at 2003 Commencement

who have reached milestones or who have decided not to return the for the coming school year. Since my retirement reception was scheduled for the following week I was did not expect anything at this event. I was pleasantly surprised when Ron Hertzler honored me with words of tribute. He went into detail about his appreciation for a letter I had written to him at the time he was invited to become part of the CD social studies team. To top it off I was given an impressive framed painting of Edward Hicks' *Peaceable Kingdom*. This is very special to me because of the theme and the fact that he was a noted local artist. I also received a genealogical computer program that has already been put to good use. I was given possession of a "golden apple" that according to the pronouncement was to be held by the person who had compiled the greatest total of years on the CD staff. I'm not sure I'll be around to personally present it to Eric, Gerald, or Jerry, or whomever, so I'll have to add a codicil to my will to take care of that rite.

I was also given a treasured gift by Ken Kabakjian who created a video in which six of my colleagues, with whom I had spent at least fifteen years, honored me with their comments. At the instigation of Christopher Dock's Director of Publications, Mary Jane Souder, my retirement was well covered in the *North Penn Reporter, Souderton Independent* and *The Perkasie-Sellersville Times Herald.* In the June 4, 2003 issue of the *News Herald* it was the feature article on the "Know Your Community" page. The writer, Susan Knight devoted considerable time in interviewing students, faculty, Principal Elaine Moyer, and me and produced

With Roland Yoder at 2003 retirement reception (Yoder designed Fraktur style diploma and made the flower arrangement.)

a masterfully crafted laudation entitled "A Living Legend Retires from Teaching."

The crowning event was the June 13 retirement reception in the Clemens Center Cafeteria. Principal Elaine Moyer and Administrative Assistant Deanie Frankenfield graciously hosted the Sunday afternoon open house. Memorabilia relating to my career and school yearbooks covering my years of service were on display. The setting was greatly enhanced by several beautiful floral arrangements by Roland Yoder and Blanche Freed provided tasty refreshments.

At three o'clock Elaine Moyer opened the more formal phase with warm words of appreciation. This was followed by an eloquent encomium by Eric Bishop in which he embellished the portrayal by a student who one time said, "Looks like Santa

With Mary Jane Detweiler
(Wife of the late Richard C. Detweiler) at
2003 retirement reception for Duane Kauffman

Claus, but sounds like God." As Eric regaled the audience he wove in some entertaining anecdotes of which several revealed a side of me that seemed quite far from being godlike. For me the climax was the sharing of nine alumni who told interesting stories and gave testimonials. I was honored by the presence of over a hundred persons, and I received many thoughtful gifts, cards and letters. The occasion, along with the other culminating developments, left me with an indescribable feeling of being loved and appreciated.

25. ADVICE TO FELLOW HIGH SCHOOL TEACHERS

What makes a successful teacher? My longevity in the classroom does not mean I have found all the answers, but I have learned some lessons along the way. In some cases they were things that worked for me. In others I recognized them as shortcomings that if corrected would have greatly enhanced my efforts. With no attempt at prioritizing, I would like to be presumptuous enough to make the following suggestions:

1. **Develop your own style.** I am not saying, "Just be yourself," because there is always the need to strive for improvement. What works for one teacher may not work for you. God has made you a unique person and if He has called you to teach, He has endowed you with the qualities you need for the challenge.

2. **Remember your own adolescent days.** A good teacher must have a capacity to empathize. One of the best ways to "walk in another person's shoes" is to recall similar experiences. Flashing back to your teenage plague of acne, pressure of peers, allure of fads, and distress of a poor grade will often provide timely insights and understanding.

3. **Be a patient encourager.** All students need encouragement. Those who perform well need it as motivation for continuing their quest for excellence. Those who are struggling need constant gestures of support that build up their self-esteem. The results of such efforts do not work miracles overnight. They produce

seedlings that need tender nourishing until fruit is borne. The teacher must be willing to hang in for the long haul, ready to cope with occasional relapses along the way.

4. **See yourself as part of the team.** Don't yield to the temptation to go it alone. You may not sense the need for support, but others may benefit tremendously from yours. On a teaching staff a spirit of camaraderie is essential. If building community is a high priority, a faculty that practices it in their relationships with each other will present a model that will be hard to ignore.

5. **Correct mistakes and be willing to apologize when necessary.** If a wrong answer is given or an inaccurate detail was presented, don't try to "bluff your way through" to save face. Integrity is of utmost importance and students have an uncanny way of recognizing phoniness. If your act of indiscretion or misunderstanding has hurt a student, apologize and ask for forgiveness. The mutual benefit of a healed relationship will pay dividends that will more than compensate for the humility it entails.

6. **Stay academically active.** A good teacher must also be a good student. Though "Publish or Perish" may be an overstatement, there is a lot to be said for being engaged in constant research that calls for problem solving and presenting theses for others to challenge. It might take the form of writing a book or articles for publication or it might mean taking graduate courses and seminars to keep up to date.

7. **Develop a passion for your subject field.** Though competence begets confidence, that is not enough. The teacher must be so absorbed in the subject that the enthusiasm results in a contagious escalating passion.

8. **Maintain a strong devotional life.** The demands of teaching call for a spiritual reserve that needs to be constantly re-supplied. It is a good practice to arrive early in the morning and spend time in your classroom in quiet meditation and prayer before the school day begins.

9. **Have an understanding of the student's world.** To communicate with students you need to meet them on their level. To understand youth one needs to understand the circle of which they are a part. Displaying an awareness of their movies, music, and heroes will go far in enhancing your credibility in the eyes of those you serve.

10. **Model your own expectations.** If you expect students to get to class on time, demonstrate promptness. If you want them to hand in their assignments on time, don't hold their tests or papers for weeks. If it is your desire that they be courteous and respectful to you and others, remember to relate to them in the same way.

11. **Recognize your bias and refrain from indoctrination.** There is no harm in having a firm point of view. There is nothing wrong in trying to steer a student so that he or she adopts it as his or her own. However care must be taken to prevent forcing your position on a student. Real education consists of assisting students to make the right choices. It is your responsibility to help the student to develop skills in clear thinking and to provide alternate perspectives for consideration.

12. **Use your gift of humor.** If a sense of humor is not an indispensable quality for a teacher, it comes very close. Though not everyone has the ability to make others laugh, most at least have the ability to put a light twist on things. I'm not sure if humor is something that can be developed, but I am convinced it is possible to discover what works and what doesn't. Good humor should grow out of the situation naturally. Canned humor borrowed from somebody else or that which is contrived, will usually fall flat and be counterproductive.

EPILOGUE

At times I have told my students, "My fondest wish for you is that you will some day find a job that brings you as much fulfillment as mine has brought me." Many persons see their work as the curse God put on Cain. I had over four wonderful decades at Christopher Dock that gave me so much satisfaction it almost felt scandalous.

With the advantage of "hindsight" I can see where I could have given more. I am aware of my many mistakes. If I could do it all over again, I might make better choices where I failed, but I would likely make other blunders where I managed well. So I am left with a clear conscience and feelings of deep gratitude. That God used me to touch lives despite my shortcomings is unfathomable and inexplicable. I will forever wonder why God bestowed so many blessings on me.

Retirement was not something I anticipated with great relief, but I will accept it gratefully. When the first weeks of the 2003–2004 school year began without me I found the adjustment difficult. I had a number of dreams about my continuing presence at CD and it didn't take a Freud or a Jung to connect them with my grief over a significant loss.

Though there are things I would like to do, I am not in a frame of mind that insists there are still things I must do. Though city traffic and airport delays have somewhat diminished the joys of travel, Naomi and I would like to retrace previous steps and explore some new worlds. Genealogy is a never-ending quest and will consume as much time and energy as I will give it. There are more ancestors and relatives to discover and previous projects to be completed and published. I would like to continue my research and writing about Amish and Amish Mennonite history. In particular, I would like to complete biographical studies of Shem Zook and Joseph W. Yoder that I have begun. Though not as intense, I plan to continue my involvement with the Franconia and Lancaster Choral Singers, Mennonites of Eastern Pennsylvania, and Perkasie Mennonite Church.

At the time of its Fiftieth Anniversary, the pulse of Christopher Dock High School is strong and even more optimism is generated by another expansion project on the horizon. The school has changed and will continue to do so as it strives to be the servant of those who sustain it. I would like to stay involved in the life of the school. I have many friends there with whom I plan to stay in touch. I look forward to assisting in organizing material for an eventual school archives and anticipate attendance at concerts, dramas, sporting events, and class reunions.

Appendix

RRR

1959   1964   1967

1975   1976   1983

Evolution
of a TEACHER

1969

1973

1974

1985

1988

1994

1996

1997

1998

2002

2003

1. "The Other Side of the Bridge"

*The following document is the content of the commencement
address I gave on June 6, 2003. Though in my concluding remarks
I said I would not be receiving a diploma, I was surprised when
I was called up and presented with an honorary copy.*

Detention was just finished and I was concluding a conversation with a student when President Andrew C. walked in with two members of his cabinet. He said, "We have a big favor to ask." I could tell that. His facial expression was the same as the time he asked me to put on that Santa Claus outfit for the Christmas Chapel. I guess he figured if he could talk me into that, he could get me to do anything! When he said they wanted me to give the commencement address I was floored. I was kind of expecting to be asked to give some input during baccalaureate. But this? This was out of my league. Heavy hitters like church leaders or college professors do this, not a high school social studies teacher.

In all honesty, I have become somewhat cynical about commencement addresses. Often they are nothing but a political platform for the speaker. Then too, I could never figure out who the audience was. The speaker's words seemed addressed to the students, yet he or she stood there speaking to the people in the pews. (Since I am going to talk to you I'm going to make sure the lectern is arranged so I face you. If the others want to eavesdrop, that's fine with me.) I often wondered if students really paid attention to what was being said or if they were already on the beach or if they were obsessed with making sure their tassel would dangle at the right angle. Really, once you've heard one, you've heard them all! *You are a wonderful class. You have been well prepared. The world is in a mess. Get out there and fix it! Bring on the diplomas and let's celebrate!* (I guess I'd better elaborate a little more!)

Why did I accept? Even if I felt inadequate and unworthy, I was greatly honored. I have had a special relationship with your class. In fact, when I agreed to return to teach another year, the only condition I set forth was that I would be one of the advisors to the senior class. Though I missed out on the fun in Connecticut, I have thoroughly enjoyed my year with you. I had a great advisor group—well mannered and properly motivated. (Sam got a little restless in chapel a few times, but I could not have wished for more).

Andrew was very persuasive and I said yes after he convinced me it was a class choice. You have quite a class president! Did you know he went on the radio and said a lot of good things about me? It was quite flattering but he did kind of get carried away. He had me teaching at this school so long it would have made me a contemporary of the Colonial schoolmaster Christopher Dock himself! Fifty years? We haven't even had our fiftieth anniversary yet! Forty-five, yes, but not fifty!

It was suggested that perhaps I would make my presentation into a farewell address. Though a little bit of this flavor might be present, I've chosen to minimize that. It's your night, not mine!

Your bridge-building theme is a great choice! Your cooperative effort culminating in the engineered masterpiece for Arts Day symbolized well your many gestures of reaching out to others. Much of this took place within your class. You built bridges of friendship for the lonely, bridges of encouragement for the struggling, bridges of conciliation when differences lead to tension, and bridges of reconciliation that helped to heal broken relationships.

Your bridge building was not limited to the C.D. campus. I was deeply moved by the chapel presentation by the thirteen who went to Honduras and helped in building bridges of hope by ministering to the disadvantaged suffering children and mothers there. I felt the same way the year before when you shared your experiences in the soup kitchens of Washington, D.C. This school year some of you built bridges as you connected with people while you pumped water in Haiti or cut firewood in Ontario. A number of you have served in youth mission programs ministering around the world. I am also aware that some of you work in homes for senior citizens or day care centers for infants and how you go beyond the call of duty as you go out of your way to relate to them in a special way. Truly, building such bridges of love is what the Christian life is all about!

Obviously, there are many applications of the bridge-building metaphor. (Perhaps by the time I'm finished, you'll think I have overdone the analogies.) To turn things around, it might be suggested that you are not just bridge-builders, but also recipients of a significant bridge built on your behalf. The founders of Christopher Dock Mennonite High School put a great deal of thought and effort into building a bridge to move students into the world of their day. Since that time many have been committed to maintaining and upgrading to deal with the challenges of a changing world. Richard Detweiler, the school's beloved first principal said, "The school must be a bridge to help students cross over *no man's land* that lay between adolescence and adulthood."

Perhaps it can be said that the original bridge was a covered bridge. Great efforts were taken to protect students from worldly elements and preserve a distinctive life style. Today the territory beyond does not seem as foreboding as in earlier days. In fact, the bridge you cross in graduation does not take you to a strange land. You've already been there and have traveled back and forth.

I am often asked, "How have students changed during the years you have been teaching? (This is usually from alumni that already know the answers and in fact are the ones responsible for the changes.) I am not quick to answer and usually "beat around the bush" with a response like "The adolescent creature has remained pretty much the same as it has always been." One thing is certain and that is that today's students are worldlier. Check out the old school yearbooks and you'll see "Beulah ain't what she used to be!" In terms of how students look, where they go and how they use their time, there is a big difference.

I am not saying today's students are less spiritual. These changes reflect new patterns in the home and church. Much of it is a response to urbanization in our local community. When the school was started over 60% of the students came from farms. Today it would be about 3%. (The first all-school social was a corn husking bee on the school property.) Then too, the Mennonite Church has shifted from isolationism and external nonconformity to wider involvement and a greater emphasis on the inner life. So it should be no surprise that mini-skirts, discothèques, malls, video arcades, and MTV have become a part of the local Mennonite youth culture.

In making another comparison, I believe that more students today are willing to take ownership for their faith and are freer to talk about their spiritual journey. The amazing level of spiritual maturity exhibited by your class in chapels and class discussion has been a challenge to me and has brought a high level of fulfillment. For those who might question this, I invite them to come for senior presentations. For us teachers what happens at this point makes it all worthwhile.

Yes, you are more urbane and cosmopolitan than the students of earlier days. But, that does not guarantee success in dealing with the pressures you will face on the other side of the bridge. Today's world has become more complex and the challenges more demanding. Up to this point you could return to the security the school provided—your classmates and teammates, teachers, guidance counselors, administration, Bob and his kitchen staff, the routine of your daily schedule. You have survived the academic rigors and qualify for graduation, but now you face the big test of applying what you have learned. Though the prospects might seem daunting, the good news is you do not have to face the new challenges alone.

I'd like to go back to the scriptural passage introduced last night. In his letter to the Romans, Paul provides wonderful encouragement. Chapter 8 Verses 31 and 32 state *"If God is for us, who can be against us? He who did not spare his own son, but gave him up for us all—how will he not also, along with him, graciously give us all things?...Who shall separate us from the love of Christ? Shall trouble or hardship or persecution or famine or nakedness or danger or sword?"* He responds by saying, *"No, in all these things we are more than conquerors through him who loved us."* He goes on in verses 38 and 39 to say *"For I am convinced that neither death nor life, neither angels nor demons, neither the present nor the future, nor any powers, neither height nor depth, nor anything else in all creation will be able to separate us from the love of God that is in Christ Jesus our Lord."* Paul identifies two different sets of challenges. The first lists seven specific hardships with which it would seem difficult to cope (trouble, hardship, persecution, famine, nakedness, danger and sword). He later goes on one of his poetic binges enumerating ten that are more obscure and even puzzling (death, life, angels, demons, the present, the future, powers, height, depth, anything in creation). I have read commentaries where each of these was interpreted and amplified but that is not necessary. Trying to dissect his literary image would be like looking at a landscape scene wondering the significance of every stone, cloud, flower, or blade of grass. The meaning is clear! You can think of every terrifying thing that this or any world can produce but not one is able to separate us from Jesus, God's ultimate bridge of love. As William Barclay said, "If God is Lord of every terror and Master of every world, of what shall we be afraid?"

If Paul were writing in our day what fearful phenomena would he identify? Perhaps it would be war and terrorism, AIDS and SARS, earthquakes and floods, corporate fraud and unjust politics, or unemployment and falling stock prices. These will present challenges that can seem overwhelming. Yet, in all of these we can be more than conquerors.

Sometimes our biggest threats are things that are not perceived in a negative light, yet their subtle pull tends to separate us from the love of Christ. The good life is fraught with many dangers. (Do you remember the story of the Billy Goats Gruff? It should be noted that after they dealt with the troublesome troll, they crossed the bridge and overindulged in the delicious grass on the other side to the point that they were quite incapacitated.) Success, wealth, prestige, and power are often trolls in disguise.

The Bible is full of many promises that God is able and willing to meet our needs and keep us safe and secure. But, we also have a part to play. He is our good shepherd, but we must stay close to hear his voice and be willing to follow.

Life on the other side of the bridge demands more responsibility for choices made. Your school experience has helped to prepare you for this. Though taking initiative is commendable, yielding to the temptation to go it alone will inevitably lead to trouble. Proverbs 3:5–6 provides the reminder to *"Trust in the Lord with all your heart and do not rely on your own understanding. In all your ways acknowledge Him and he will make straight your paths."* In his epistle James put it well when he said, *"Draw near to God and he will draw near to you."*

Drawing near to God can take various forms. Cultivating a close communion with God through Bible reading and prayer is essential. But God often deals with us in our relationships with other people. I urge you to take seriously the importance of continuing to be a part of a Christian community, be it a church or a student Christian fellowship on the college campus. The strength and direction derived from this type of encouragement and accountability will be invaluable.

As a teacher, one of my greatest sources of joy and satisfaction has been seeing students develop after they have crossed the graduation bridge. I'm often amazed, and reminded of my own lack of faith, when I see miraculous changes and growth resulting from good choices made. On the other hand, one of the greatest disappointments comes from observing students who had their spiritual acts together and represented the very best in C.D. students, cast their earlier values aside as they plunge into the American mainstream. It seems in most cases, it happened because they tried to go it alone.

Yes, you have built bridges and have even laid some planks on the one you are crossing tonight. If you are faithful to your call much more bridge building lies ahead. I would like to conclude with a poem by Will Allen Dromgoole. I think is appropriate. On the surface it might seem to apply more to me, but the theme speaks of each generation's responsibilities to its successors.

> *An old man, going a lone highway*
> *Came, at the evening, cold and gray,*
> *To a chasm, vast, and deep, and wide,*
> *Through which was flowing a sullen tide.*
> *The old man crossed in the twilight dim;*
> *The sullen stream had no fears for him;*
> *But he turned, when safe on the other side,*
> *And built a bridge to span the tide.*
> *"Old man," said a fellow pilgrim, near,*
> *"You are wasting strength with building here:*
> *Your journey will end with the ending day."*
> *You never again must pass this way;*
> *You have crossed the chasm, deep and wide—*
> *Why build you the bridge at eventide?"*
> *The builder lifted his old gray head:*
> *"Good friend, in the path I have come," he said,*
> *"There followeth after me today*
> *A youth, whose feet must pass this way.*
> *That chasm, that has been naught to me,*

To that fair-haired youth may a pitfall be.
He, too, must cross in the twilight dim;
Good friend, I am building the bridge for him."

Last year I started across the bridge to retirement on the other side. I was not running, but I was well on my way. Admittedly I was somewhat cautious. I heard familiar voices and kept looking back. Your gentle nudging helped me to decide to delay my crossing. It was a good decision. I had a great year.

Now there is no turning back. Tonight you are crossing the bridge and I am going along. (Put on gown) I'm graduating too. No, I'll not get a diploma or a degree, but I am graduating into another interval of life. (Note—this green gown with my white hair represents our school colors very well!)

To the school community I say *farewell*. To my colleagues on the faculty and staff, to students present and past, to parents, and friends—thanks for letting me be on the team. Thanks for the trust and support you have given me. I have been richly blessed.

2. "Why I Am Opposed to the Letter Grading System"

*The following document was a presentation
I made January 11, 1973 in an open forum of students
and teachers. Frankly, I do not recall how it was accepted
or that it precipitated any significant response.*

Let me describe the action! The teachers are on the attack! Mr. White throws a good sneaky surprise notebook check. Mr. Brown roars through with a terrific pop quiz. Mr. Green smashes in with a true-false test that leaves a trail of sparks! Mrs. Black barrels through with a booming 250-point quota for chapter seven. Miss Gray chips in with a telling essay exam! Mrs. Blue charges in with her five points off for spelling! But hold it folks! The students are charging back!

Bob bursts through with his crib notes and heaves himself into the fray! Sue sneaks through on the left side with her deadly plagiarism. Sandy bucks past with spelling words on her palm. Joe eludes the defenders with a classic job of apple-polishing. Bill comes thundering through in fine style with a sizzling con job on his essay and cross-eyed Tom slashes out with a daring exhibition of copying answers from his neighbor's paper!

This would all be funny if it were only a game. Unfortunately, it's a battle! To some it's a matter of life or death! I am not opposed to evaluation. I am not opposed to prods of encouragement. I am opposed to the letter grading system. Here are ten of my reasons why:

1. **It is poor motivation for learning.** Grades seem to be the school's bananas that are used to train student monkeys to push or pull a certain lever. Grades tend to become ends in themselves and students often become so involved in concentrating on marks that genuine learning does not occur. The most legitimate motive for real learning is the joy of discovery. Alas, the ruts are so deep and the conditioning so complete that the concept of true learning is too vague to be recognized!

2. **It encourages using wrong evaluation criteria.** The system tends to be based on comparing students with other students in the group. The famous *bell curve* is a good case in point. This is not reliable since the general level of the entire group may be either high or low. Even more important, it would seem that instead of evaluating students by comparing them with other students, it would be better to compare them with their past performance and their own ability. This type of evaluation is not encouraged by the letter grade system!

3. **It is too vague.** A good grading system conveys meaning to students and parents. The letter grade is so vague it is almost meaningless. What does a (C) mean? (Good? Fair? Average? All four?) In what respects is the performance fair or poor? Today education is becoming more individualized. It would stand to reason that evaluation must also be geared more to a particular student. This calls for far more than a letter grade.

4. **It is not used consistently by the various teachers.** It is common knowledge that some teachers are "hard" while others are "easy" graders. This is no laughing

matter when once considers that many courses are selected on this basis and that the difference between a B- and a C+ may mean whether one makes the honor roll or not.

5. It leads to undesirable by-products of keen competition. In short, it leads students into the temptation of dishonesty and encourages them to take short-cuts to meet questionable requirements. It is true that competition is an incentive and brings out the best in some. By the same token, it also calls forth the worst in some. It is true that this type of "survival-of-the-fittest" competition is much like what goes on in the outside adult world. But, does that mean that our grading system is right merely because it adheres to the patterns of our other life systems? Then too, this competition contributes heavily to the chronic disease of "Whadjugit" which has left a wake of dashed hopes and broken friendships.

6. It discourages low-ability students. Many feel that an occasional D or F will shock a student into mending his ways. That may be true for the bright student who was "goofing off." It is not true in the case of the struggling low-ability student. A steady barrage of low marks will not provide encouragement, but rather, on the other hand, breeds discouragement and futility which often culminates in a state of depression, feelings of inferiority, or dropping out.

7. It discourages a good student from taking a course in which he might not succeed. Good, well-rounded students often have an area of weakness. It just might happen he has a sense of curiosity that stimulates interest in a course in his area of weakness. The fear of an F or even a C will cause him to shy away from such course.

8. The system is often used by teachers as punitive action. The system is intended for the evaluation of a performance. Some teachers yield to the temptation of using this opportunity to punish a student for being tardy, skipping class, or forgetting his homework papers. These acts should not be overlooked but, in most cases, should be dealt with separately rather than being a factor in giving a letter grade for the performance.

9. The system tends to categorize students as to which ones have certain rights and which ones do not. It gives the "powers that be" the occasion to arbitrarily give some students privileges while denying others the same. One student wears a halo as valedictorian because of academic achievement without many questions asked about values and attitudes. Another boy stupidly tries to take a course in physics and is rewarded by being bounced from the basketball team for not meeting eligibility standards.

10. The cry that colleges require letter grades for admission is a fallacy. This oft-repeated justification for hanging on to the letter grade system is no longer true. Within the last several years, colleges have begun to change their admission policy. Greater priority is being placed on non-academic criteria in college selections.

Two reasons for keeping this system are that it's traditional and it's convenient. Is this traditional convenience worth its bad effects? I don't think so! I have not worked on developing a perfect substitute. Several options or combinations would be acceptable. The system of "Superior," "Pass," "No credit" appeals to me. I would like to see it fortified with regular narrative reports from the teacher and frequent conferences involving teachers, students, and parents.

3. "The Rebel's Code"

In the spring of 1968 I gave a chapel presentation. Someone from the Mennonite Publishing House happened to be in the audience and was responsible for having the speech printed in the With *magazine. Later I gave permission for its use by* Teens Today *a periodical published by the Nazarene Publishing House. At the time Herald Press celebrated their twenty-fifth anniversary of* With *they reprinted the article since it reflected the times of its original appearance. The readers will no doubt notice that at this point I was still consistently using the male gender in the words I chose.*

Rebellion is a symbol of the times. Revolt is everywhere. All of us are caught up in it in one way or another, consciously or unconsciously. Many oppose rebellion and are incensed to be labeled as rebels. Yet that is what they are, because they are rebelling against the rebellion. We are all rebels! We differ only in our motives, the degrees of our protests, and the forms our rebellion takes.

Rebellion in itself is neither good nor evil. It must be viewed in terms of motivation and the legitimacy of the form it takes. Progress does not result from maintaining the status quo. Rebels are needed who are not afraid to stick out their necks. Tensions will likely result. But tensions are a sign of movement, and only time will reveal the direction of the movement.

On the other hand, revolt often tends to cloud the issues and impedes progress. Sometimes a successful revolt solves one problem but gives rise to two others equally as serious. Today's rebellion is associated with youth, for it is a normal phase in development. However, with independence comes responsibility. In an attempt to bring together rebellion and responsibility, I have constructed what I call "The Rebel's Code." It contains ten guidelines for rebelling.

1. **Make sure the trouble does not lie within you.**

    Often outward displays of rebellion are results of inner guilt feelings and have nothing to do with any prevailing external condition. This is a normal human reaction, and the person involved is often unaware of the real motivation of his actions.

    Many rebels only need to get something out of their system. Maybe a good scream now and then is good for one's mental health, but one must make sure that giving vent to one's frustrations does not harm himself or somebody else.

    Often on the basketball court, the player whose mistake puts his team behind rebels by breaking the rules or taking it out on the "ref." It is good to sit down and ask the basic question, *what makes me tick?* The ancient philosopher put it, "Know thyself."

2. **Make sure you understand the factors that have led to the problem.**

    Many problems, when reviewed carefully from every possible angle, have a way of seeming much less significant. Problems have a way of becoming exaggerated. Often judgments concerning issues are not based on reality, but on rumors or someone's opinion.

    So it is important to look at the whole picture. The rebel owes it to those he is rebelling against to try to look at the problem from their angle. Often one who does not clearly understand the problem finds he is merely fighting symptoms instead of getting to the real cause.

3. **Make sure you have a cause and you haven't merely jumped on a bandwagon.**

One who fights a cause must be sure he has a real principle. Often glittering generalities such as peace and freedom are given as the motivating factors. Many hide behind a screen of ambiguity.

Often a person claims to be rebelling in the name of freedom to express his individuality. The truth is he's only rationalizing his desire to follow a certain fad. Nonconformity can so easily become conformity. A desire to "be in" can be understood as another human trait. It's natural to want to be accepted by the group. But let's not kid ourselves into thinking we're fighting for some great noble cause.

4. **Rebel rationally, not just emotionally.**

One who rebels must keep his cool. Group behavior has a tendency to become irrational. People in a moment of excitement, urged on by others do things they would not ordinarily do. Many causes have been defeated because emotionalism caused the crusaders to go to extremes.

How many times has the juvenile officer, or the school principal heard the words, "I just got carried away and couldn't help myself."

5. **Direct your rebellion toward the cause of your trouble.**

The person who takes out his hostilities on the innocent is a coward. If it is a real solution that he wants, a direct confrontation is the only way to deal with the matter. How much sense does it make for a boy to rebel against his mother, who has compelled him to eat his oatmeal, by going out and beating up a small kid on the way to school? How much sense does it make for a boy whose father has just refused to give him the keys to the family car, to go to school and be a troublemaker for the teacher?

6. **Consider established laws and rules of behavior.**

    Local laws and codes of behavior are often firmly established. They are usually products of careful thought and have endured for long periods of time. Policies such as these should not be taken lightly.

    There may be a time for the principle of a "higher law" to be invoked and for "man's law" to be defied. This is an extreme move. It is the extremely exceptional case. The big question is, "Whose judgment is worthy of making such a decision? Before one decides to defy established policies, he must be ready to abide by the consequences. For Martin Luther King, Jr. it meant jail. For John Hus it meant death. For you it might mean something else.

7. **Keep the lines of communication open.**

    Many clashes result from misunderstandings. Often irreparable schisms can be avoided if both parties are willing to give the other side a hearing. Today much is being said about the generation gap. Adults berate the reckless, supposedly immoral youth, and the youth complain about the lack of understanding and the double standard of adults. Both are to blame. The real problem is that the two are not on speaking and working terms.

    In international matters, breaking off diplomatic relations is an act just short of war. In most cases war inevitably follows. And how much has ever been solved by war?

8. **Be positive and constructive.**

    A good rebel is more than a muckraker or a gadfly. A muckraker digs up dirt and filth. He sees the evil and points it out. This can be an important contribution, but merely discovering it and publicizing it does not in itself clean things up.

    The gadfly (or common horsefly) is one who annoys —"always on someone's back." The gadfly does not make the horse a better creature except giving him stronger tail muscles as a result of the constant exercise he encourages.

Mass demonstrations have their place. At least they provide a person with the chance to stand up and be counted. Which will do more good? To march, sit, kneel, squat, or chant for more civil rights for the Afro-American or to invite African foreign students into your home for Christmas vacation or to choose an Afro-American for a college roommate or go into the city ghetto with a Voluntary Service group to put principles of love into practice? It's your choice.

9. **If you see you are wrong, don't keep rebelling just to save face.**

Many causes that were considered just have been proved otherwise. Often this realization comes slowly. But when it comes, what then? Imagine how humiliating it must have been for the Apostle Paul to minister to the needs of those he previously had tried to kill and to condemn those who had been his old friends.

Saving face seems so important, and eating crow is so hard, but this is what "separates the men from the boys."

10. **Rebel with all your mind, heart, and strength.**

If all the other nine "commandments" have been kept and the cause is worthwhile, it is worth some sacrifices and total effort. Don't be a "fair weather" rebel who fights only when it is convenient or when it does require sacrifice. Go all out!

A Christian who takes his calling seriously will be a rebel. Christ was a rebel, and they crucified him for it. Paul and his aide were once accused of "turning the world upside down." So go ahead and rebel. But don't forget the rebel's code.

4. "My Reactions to the Proposed Master Plan"

*In the 1976–1977 school year, persons were given
the opportunity to respond to several campus master plans.
What follows was my response.*

1. **I feel the campus concept should be retained.** Our educational philosophy can be best implemented in a setting that provides a sanctuary from the larger hectic, mechanical, impersonal world. Various centers should be developed for subject fields such as art-music, math-science, home economics, business education, and social studies—English. Concerns such as carrying equipment, getting cold or wet, or insufficient time between classes, are not important enough,, in the final analysis, to merit having one big building, or for that matter, one big complex connected with "breezeways,"

2. **I do not favor one centrally located media center.** A degree of centralization is needed for organization and efficiency. However, in my opinion, decentralization better provides for multi-media needs. Each department should have its own library and audio-visual aids. Multi-media materials should be centrally catalogued to facilitate inter-departmental use.

3. **I feel the circular drive pattern should be retained.** This plan does not pose an absolute restriction to expansion. Moving the baseball field opens an area for possible development. Being

able to circumnavigate the campus would aid in traffic control. In my opinion, Plan #2 provides utility, order and beauty.

4. **A student-center should be provided**
    The following should be included:
    - (a) Lounge area with tables for card games, phono graph, and television etc.
    - (b) Recreation room with shuffleboard, pool tables, ping-pong etc.
    - (c) Student store
    - (d) Conference rooms for student officers and Campus Senate
    - (e) Snack bar

    School is not only preparation for life, but school **is** life! Socialization is very important in the development of the "whole child." The trend toward "open periods" should not be ignored. The student-center would provide a place for socialization during the student's free time" (lunch periods, non-compulsory study halls, and activities periods.)

5. **The gymnasium should be expanded more than the present plans provide.** In the long range, in order to provide for physical development and recreation of our students, we should add:
    - (a) Additional basketball and volleyball courts
    - (b) More bleacher space
    - (c) Better lavatory facilities
    - (d) Better locker rooms
    - (e) Bowling facilities
    - (f) Heated swimming pool

6. **Grebel Hall should be renovated and made less "barn like."** Some partitions should be removed to combine smaller classrooms into larger ones. Teachers' conference rooms should be provided and classrooms altered to provide workshops for learn-

ing. I recommend that the media center headquarters remain, but that the Conference Archives be moved.

7. A new Administration Building be provided. The idea of changing our present "Administration Building" into a museum does not appear as a joke to me. I like the idea, and I feel the archives should be housed there.

8. Outdoor toilet and drinking facilities should be provided. These should be located near the athletic fields.

9. A campus "woods" should be started and maintained. Several acres with a good variety of trees and other natural growth would not only be a step toward filling conservation and recreation needs, but would add considerably to overall campus beauty. Picnic facilities should be included.

10. Better facilities should be provided for the driver education program. This should include garage space for the cars, a paved area for "in-car" instruction and a classroom with simulated driving equipment.

This is the time to dream and not a time to pinch pennies! Master planning is no irreversible commitment! Realistic financing will eventually determine implementation, but let's not have history say of us, "they were shortsighted."

Sincerely,   S. Duane Kauffman

5. "The Big Little Man of C.D."

*In thinking about presenting a tribute to Roland Yoder
at a special retirement banquet in the spring of 1999,
I chose the format of a ballad to express my sentiments.
Words cannot express the inestimable contributions
he made, but I believe I captured a few
of the significant gifts he gave us.*

Refrain
He's short of height; but he's full of might.
His spirit is alive and free.
His life gives light so that others can see.
He's the big, little man of CD.

Come gather 'round me people; there are thoughts I'd like to share.
I'll tell you of a teacher who was born in Delaware.
Perhaps by now you've guessed that Roland Yoder is his name.
Without his legacy, our school would not be the same.

In the cozy Yoder farmhouse in the fall of thirty-five
Roland made his entrance and was very much alive.
Just before the doctor made his exit through the door,
Bertha said, "Please wait, I think I'll have one more."

In the Greenwood Christian Day School the pupils often played
While "Rolie" took his crayons and pretty pictures made.
And when the other local lads went walking with their dogs
The oldest son of Albert looked for crickets under logs.

At EMC this prodigy majored in biology.
A Zelathian and Avian was he.
Though D. Ralph kept him busy throughout the entire year
He still found time to court his Dottie dear.

In Florida and Oregon his teaching role began.
Then in the year of sixty, Pennsylvania got its man.
With Melissa and Yolanda they made Harleysville their home,
But something in his blood made him always want to roam.

London, Rome, and Bogotá; Australia's wild outbacks,
Addis, Athens, Anchorage, Oslo and Halifax;
He counts his miles by thousands on the bus or in the air.
Look at the map and name it. You can be sure that he's been there.

His great rapport with students has served him very well.
He even took his turn as yearbook mentor for a spell.
In planning banquet settings he led them to new heights,
And all who attended were inspired by awesome sights.

Biology and chemistry he taught with all his heart.
Yet his special contributions were in the field of art.
Students gladly took his course on lawn and garden care
While his overflowing classes took their pictures here and there.

But life in the classroom is not always a breeze.
Some days he spends much time just looking for his keys.
Once a chalk eraser actually got up and went,
And lost cameras and clay give him much cause to lament.

It's his belief that teaching and learning should be fun.
So the air is filled with laughter caused by a subtle pun.
With a gentle pat and kindly smile he sends them on their way,
And his words of affirmation often made a student's day.

Bradford Pear trees not withstanding, the CD campus is a wonder!
Without his aesthetic touch we are only left to ponder
How bleak and uninviting our space would really be.
Who deserves the credit? Yes, indeed, it is he.

The impact of his character goes far beyond our school.
With tours, church and home his hours certainly are full.
His multitude of friends that can be found anywhere
Would say his greatest gift is his propensity to care.

And now the time has come for us to say our good-byes.
It's hard to keep the tears from welling in our eyes.
But diplomas and aromas still yield their memories dear,
And the presence of his spirit will forever linger here.

6. "The Ballad of Duane Kauffman"

The following song was composed and performed by Jerry Yoder
at my retirement reception on June 15, 2003. He put words to
a song that I often performed called The "Friendly Beasts."
The surprise ending refers to another song I frequently
sang entitled "The Cat Came Back."

Kauffman our colleague, a man we now fete,
    came to CD in '58.
The school was young and he was too.
    His hair was cut into a crew.

Serving his country in 1-W,
    doing whatever he was asked to do.
The first few years were pretty rough.
    Franconia Cowboys can be rather tough.

Health and Phys. Ed. Classes suited him just fine.
    Coaching and "reffing" took more of his time
"The Art of Clear Thinking", a quarter course theme,
    bowling in class and on the faculty team.

Teaching the Senate parliamentary rules,
    giving his students researcher's tools,
Finding branches on family trees,
    all the while tending his family of bees.

Sleeping students, you'd better beware,
    Kauffman will find you and give you a scare.
Yardstick bangs waste can or slaps top of desk,
    anything to keep you from getting your rest.

"Know that word. That's a good word," he'd say,
    "You might see it on a test some day.
"Bear with me now, I've got more to say,"
    and Beulah could show up most any day.

His Civil War songs were always well met,
    singing the bass part in the faculty quartet,
Ballads from Scotland, Appalachian melodies,
    Duane and his guitar were sure to please.

Sabbaticals were always times to retool,
    Europe and Scotland, St. Andrews school,
Research and writing historical books,
    sometimes returning changing his looks.

Serving on committees and task forces too,
    hundreds and thousands of extra things to do.
Always helping us to get to the point,
    meetings kept moving in Kauffman's joint.

Duane is leaving us after 45 years.
    It's okay if you feel you have to shed some tears,
He's moving on, heading further down the track,
    one thing is for sure,

THIS CAT'S NOT COMING BACK

7. "A Force to Be Reckoned With"

*The following song was written and sung by 2003 graduate Bonnie
Doherty as a tribute at my retirement reception in June 2003.
I have it on videocassette and prize it very highly.*

Where do I begin?
Losing a friend is never easy.
You've been a rock in a stormy sea.
Not just for me.
Your roots here run deep
And we'll go out and make our way in this world.
How many times have you heard that?
How many times have you heard
"I can't."
And you're the one to say
"Oh, but you can.
You can do all things through Him who gives you strength."
Like the ocean billows against the shore
You are.
Like the thunder clashes over mountains
You are.
And like the little bird that doesn't know the meaning
     of giving up
You are a force to be reckoned with.

Where do you go from here?
Wonder if you're scared.
Maybe just excited
About your new adventure.
Just remember, you're never alone.
Like the ocean billows against the shore
You are.
Like the thunder crashes over mountains
You are.
And like the little bird that doesn't know the meaning
   of giving up
You are a force to be reckoned with.
You are a force to be reckoned with.

**With Bonnie Doherty at
the 2003 Commencement**